Candle Magick Divination
Good Luck - Good Fortune

By Dragonstar

Inner Light Publications

CANDLE MAGICK DIVINATION:
GOOD LUCK -- GOOD FORTUNE
Secrets of Your Future Revealed In The Flame

by Dragonstar

Timothy G. Beckley, Editorial Director
Assistant Editor, Carol Rodriguez

Free Catalog from:
Inner Light Publications, Box 753,
New Brunswick, NJ 08903 www.webufo.net

Candle Magick Divination

CONTENTS

Candle Magick Divination

The Magickal Flames Of Dragonstar

Candle Magick Divination

Introduction
By Tim Swartz

What is Magick? Is there a force in the universe that can influence our lives in ways that can't be explained by science? Is this force a separate energy, or another aspect of our own ultimate reality? And, is this ultimate reality malleable by our minds?

These are questions that have been asked throughout the centuries when dealing with the unknown. It has been suggested by those more spiritual in nature, that our entire universe is actually an infinite sea of energy that our consciousness keeps in order. Without us, the universe would not, could not, exist.

We see around us every day the reality of our minds made real. Everything that we have in the material world first started as a simple thought, an idea. This shows us that thoughts have power. This amazing power has the ability to shape and mold our reality into something that it wasn't before. Our world, our universe, is composed entirely of thoughts made real.

This could be the worst kept secret of the true meaning of our existence. Philosophers and Shamans said it first. And now, scientists have started to come around to this same idea with Quantum physics and other forms of modern science. Our consciousness, our thoughts not only control reality, they are reality.

This is the fundamental tenet of the author, Dragonstar, who is the current living Dragonstar of *The Mystical Lodge of Dragonstar*. This ancient school of mystical knowledge claims a lineage that stretches back thousands of years to what we know today as the ancient civilization of Atlantis.

This civilization maintained an order of priest/scientists that were scattered across the planet to bring spiritual teachings and science to other, newly emerging societies. These emissaries of Atlantis brought the first vestiges of civilization to a young mankind. When Atlantis was destroyed and sunk beneath the dark waters of the ocean, it also sank the rest of the world back into a dark age of anarchy.

Fortunately, many of the priests from Atlantis survived in other lands untouched by the cataclysm that destroyed their home. These messengers, with their mystical teachings and science, gave mankind the knowledge to once again set themselves on the correct path of spiritual and scientific reawakening. This book takes this ancient knowledge and puts it in a language understood by modern society. This knowledge is now yours. Use it wisely and cause no harm to others.

Candle Magick Divination

Chapter One
The Art of Candle Magick

Since earliest time, humankind has equated fire with Divinity. The Sun was regarded as a Deity, and fire was one of its expressions. Primitives noticed that when the body was alive, it was warm. And when cold, it was dead. They surmised that fire must also be the essence of life.

No one can definitively say when fire was discovered by humans, nor when it was domesticated. Originally, fires may have been carried from areas devastated by volcanoes, or from fires started by lightning during thunderstorms. Coals had to be guarded carefully and carried from place to place as fire was needed. Imagine what a luxury it must have seemed when someone figured out how to make fire. Warmth, cooked food, and light suddenly became readily available. Surely this was magickal to early people. In honor of the new treasure, the new magick, many fire celebrations came into existence.

It has been eons of this unconscious idea which is behind the use of fire in worship and ritual. Igniting a fire triggers a primal, prehistoric part of our souls. It is an act of magick.

When done for religious or spiritual purposes, that ancient idea sets in motion powerful forces. Fire and light have great power to move the soul and thereby stir the forces of magick. As well, candle burning has roots stretching back to ancient times as a part of both religious ceremonies and magical rites.

One of the easiest of magickal arts which comes under the heading of natural magic is candle burning. It is simple because it employs little ritual and few ceremonial artifacts. The theatrical props of candle magic can be purchased at any department store and its rituals can be practiced in any quiet room.

Most of us have performed our first act of candle magic by the time we are two years old. Blowing out the candles on our birthday cake and making a wish is pure candle magick.

This childhood custom is based on the three magickal principles of concentration, will power and visualization. In simple terms, the child who wants his wish to come true has to concentrate (blow out the candles), visualize the end result (make a wish) and hope that it will come true (will power).

Candle Magick Divination

Early Candles

Necessity is the mother of invention and early candles sometimes took rather bizarre forms to make use of available resources. As man has spread himself across the globe, candles in all shapes and forms have followed to light the way.

There is no historical record of the first candles used by man, however clay candle holders dating from the fourth century B.C. have been found in Egypt. Early Chinese and Japanese candles were made with wax derived from insects and seeds molded in paper tubes. Wax skimmed from boiling cinnamon was the basis of tapers for temple use in India.

The first known candle in America dates to the first century A.D. Native Americans burned oily fish (candlefish) wedged into a forked stick. Early missionaries in the southwestern United States boiled the bark of the Cerio tree and skimmed the wax. Settlers in New England used the same technique to obtain wax from Bayberries. To this day Bayberry candles are made the same way.

Tallow, made by rendering animal fat was another common candle making material. Because of its odor, beeswax was preferred although more expensive. The advent of paraffin in the 1800's made tallow obsolete, and it is rarely used in candles anymore.

Candle making as we know it began in the 13th century when traveling candlers went door to door making dipped tapers from their clients tallow or beeswax (wealthier clients). The first use of molds for candle making was in 15th century Paris.

Before the 16th century, candles were made of tallow or sometimes lamps containing oil with a fibre of some sort as a wick. They often smoked, sputtered and smelled. Only the rich and elite could afford the more rare and costly beeswax candles. The Renaissance of candle crafting was during the 19th century. Candle molding machines were developed in the first half of the century. In 1811 pioneer work lead to the development of stearin. The braided wick was introduced in 1825. This year also saw the manufacture of stearic acid (a candle additive used to harden and opacify wax).

Paraffin development began in 1830. A continuous wicking machine was invented in 1834. Mordanting of wicks was a major breakthrough in 1834. Mordanting causes the burned end of the wick to curl outside of the flame zone where it turns to ash. Manufactured paraffin was introduced in 1850, providing an alternative to tallow. In 1854 paraffin and stearin were combined to create stronger candles, very similar to those we use today.

Candle Magick Divination

Colored candles as we know them today have only been common for the past thirty years. Prior to this, most candles available were of the utilitarian white variety. The dyes used to color wax must be oil soluble and are therefore only available from limited sources.

Plant based colors were difficult to extract, and were only capable of coloring wax to the warmer hues of the spectrum, (red, orange & yellow). Pigment dyes were another limited source of color. They are extremely finely ground minerals, so finely ground that it was again, extremely difficult with the technology that preceded the early 19th century to produce color candles.

For example: Although copper carbonate was available, the ability to grind it finely enough to remain suspended in wax as a (blue-green) color was impossible before the early 1800's. As well, aniline dyes were not available until quite recently. These dyes derived from coal and oil, and have only been available since the late 19th century.

No one really knows when man first used candles and fire for the purpose of magickal rituals. Lighting a candle is like bringing Divine Power into a situation. Of course, if things worked that easily, we'd only have to strike a match to get the magick flowing. Though the urge behind it is simple, making the magick do what you want takes more. Our minds have evolved considerably since those ancient times. Our magick must evolve, also. What makes candle magick so popular is its simplicity, availability, and adaptability. Candles are easy to get and use. The ways of using them are flexible. They can be adapted to almost any tradition or religion. They can be employed for almost any intention.

Probably the single most important influence on modern candle magick originated in the 1940s with the book: ***Master Book of Candle-Burning***, a pamphlet written by Henri Gamache in 1942. Advertised in black-owned newspapers like the ***Chicago Defender*** in the 1940s, this book can still be found today in a number of mail-order spiritual supply catalogues.

This work was one of the first mass produced books to offer detailed instructions on how to burn candles for every purpose. The chapters include information on how to select candles, anoint them, arrange them on an altar, and engage in what the author refers to as "fire worship."

Along the way Gamache presents a garland of anthropological tidbits about folk-magical practices from Canada, Europe, Africa, and the Malayan Peninsula, making this book a fascinating and influential document.

Candle Magick Divination

Candles used for magickal purposes can come in every shape, size and color. Some spells call for certain types and colors, but the final decision on what candle is right for your needs is entirely up to you.

Candle Magick Divination

Figure And Seven Day Candles

In addition to plain candles, spiritual suppliers, as early as the 1930s, provided figure candles for special uses. Most of these styles are still manufactured. Among the most popular are: **The black cat** – black for gambler's luck. **Man and woman side by side with two wicks (bride and groom)** – red for passion, reconciliation, white to attract new love or sanctify married fidelity.

Nude embracing couple (Lovers) – red for sexual passion. **Nude male figure or nude female figure** – red for love and passion, black for harm or revenge. **Male or female genital organs** – control of the sexual behavior of another; red to induce passion, black to control their ability to perform, blue to limit their sexual interest to the practitioner only.

The lucky hand – green for gambler's luck. **Keys and a book on a flaming cross (master key crucifix candle)** – white for spiritual purity and insight, black for personal power and conjure work. **Standing devil** – red for commanding lust and sex, green for collecting money owed or for gambler's luck, black for doing harm to an enemy. **Seated Baphomet or Sabbatic Goat** – red for lust spells, black for worship of bestial or Satanic forces.

The skull – black for meditation on death or for gambler's luck. **Seven knob wishing candle** – burned on seven days, for seven different wishes or for seven-fold strength on the same wish – white for healing, black to do evil, green for money, red for love.

The Catholic religion practices the ritual of the novena with its nine-day candle. In early candle magick there is the seven-day candle, sometimes referred to by older practitioners as the "Seven-day vigil candle," due to its being burned over the course of seven days, while one watches and waits for signs. The seven-day vigil candle was reserved for difficult cases or ongoing situations.

Candle Magick historian Catherine Yronwode writes that there are four types of seven-day candles used in the old African American practice of hoodoo.

The candle is divided by seven needles or pins: To make one, take a regular or jumbo-size candle and seven needles or pins. Poke the needles into the candle, dividing it into seven equal parts. Write your wish (or seven wishes) on a piece of paper. Turn the paper 90 degrees sideways and write your full name over the wish or wishes seven times, crossing and covering the previous writing with your name. Place the paper under the candle. Dress the candle with an appropriate oil such as olive.

Candle Magick Divination

Burn it for seven nights, pinching it out, not blowing it out, each time a needle falls. Save the needles when they fall. When the last needle falls, stick the needles into the paper in the form of two X patterns surrounding one double-cross pattern, (that has two lines crossing one upright line).

Dispose of the ritual remains in an appropriate way : Bury the paper and any leftover wax under your doorstep if your intention is to draw something or someone to you. Throw the paper and wax away at a crossroads, in running water, or in a graveyard if the intention is to get rid of something or someone.

The seven knob candle: There have been ads for these candles under the name: *The Famous 7-Knob Wishing Candle*, dating back at least to the 1930s. They are mentioned favorably in Henri Gamache's *Master Book of Candle Burning*, and they are very popular in the African-American community, which seems to indicate that they are efficacious.

Seven-knob candles generally come in four colors, with the usual symbolism implied (white for blessing or wishing, red for love or sex, green for money or gambling luck, black for destruction or revenge). Carve a brief wish on each knob – either the same wish seven times or seven different wishes, one per knob. Dress the candle with an appropriate oil. Burn it for seven nights, pinching it out, not blowing it out, each time a knob is gone.

The seven charm sortilage candle: This is a hand-made candle that contains seven tiny metal charms (milagros or ex-votos) inside, which are revealed one per day as you burn the candle down over the course of seven days. It is more common in Latin America than in the United States. Often the charms are religious as well as lucky, and they may include a cross, an angel, the powerful hand of God, a man's head, a woman's head, etc.

The seven-wishes glass-encased candle: This style of seven-day candle only became popular from the 1970s onward. It is made with seven layers of wax in different colors, poured into a tall, narrow glass container. Burn one layer each day with appropriate prayers or wishes. It's interesting to note that this is the same size and shape of candle which the Catholics call a novena candle. Novena candles are designed to burn for nine days while a series of votary prayers are made. It is not customary to dress them with magical oils, nor is color-symbolism an important part of their lore. The use of such candles is widespread in Catholic Latin America; as well as in the pseudo-Catholic African-Caribbean religion known as Santeria.

Candle Magick Divination

Glass-Encased Candles

During the 1970s and 1980s, Cuban immigrants, both Catholics and Santeros, entered the United States in great numbers and a merger between hoodoo and Catholic-Santeria candle burning traditions was effected. Although special-use figural candles are still very popular with African-Americans, the old Jewish-style offertory candles have been replaced to a certain extent by seven-day vigil candles modeled after the tall, glass-enclosed Catholic-style novena candles.

The one thing that sets seven-day hoodoo candles apart from true Catholic novena candles is that the latter bear colorful paper saint image labels and the former are decorated with one-color line-art and hand-lettered text silk-screened directly onto the glass. The text and images found on seven-day candles are typically the same as those used in hoodoo formula for anointing oils, including Fast Luck, Uncrossing, Compelling, and Money House Blessing.

The evolving form of hoodoo candles has not greatly affected their traditional system of color symbolism, although under the influence of Santeria's Catholic heritage, which invokes the brown-robed Saint Anthony as the finder of lost things and returner of lost lovers, brown candles, formerly used for court cases, are now also employed for the return of that which is lost.

Glass containers make it easy to pour two, three, and even seven-layer candles, which led to the development of multi-color symbolism. Probably the most popular of the multi-color glass-encased 7-day vigil candles is the red-and-black reversible candle for returning evil to the one who sent it.

This is simply a modification of the old standby two-color free-standing altar candle called **Double Action**, which is still manufactured. However, other multi-colored candles are only found in glass-encased form, among them the seven-color Lucky Prophet Buddha Brand All Purpose Novena Candle which grants "7 desires" to the user.

The practice of dressing candles with anointing oils and herbs had to be modified considerably to accommodate the new seven-day vigil candles. Since the sides of a glass-encased candle cannot be rubbed, it is now customary for the retailer rather than the user to dress the candle. This is done by poking holes into the top of the candle with a nail (preferably a coffin nail) and then dripping the oil into these holes, sometimes finishing off the top with symbolically colored glitter.

Candle Magick Divination

This technique leaves the customer in danger of spilling the oil while carrying the candle home, so in many stores the dressed candle is covered with a plastic sandwich bag held in place by a rubber band.

The introduction of glass-encased candles also made changes necessary in spells designed to be worked over a length of time. The old pin or needle measuring technique cannot be used on glass-encased candles, so timed burning or measuring the glass into sections with a marking-pen has taken the place of needles or pins among people who prefer the glass-encased candles.

This serves to weaken the practitioner's involvement in the spell, however, because there are no pins or needles left over to make the crosses and double crosses prescribed in the older workings. A glass-encased candle spell therefore takes on a slightly "ritual" or "religious" tone, in that one's desires and wishes are expected to do the work alone, as contrasted to an offertory candle spell, in which the manipulation of magical objects, candle, flame, paper, and needles or pins, is integral to doing the job.

In recent years, an influx of Mexican, Guatemalan, and Salvadoran immigrants to the United States has led to the increased marketing of Catholic saint novena candles, and on occasion one may even find the Guatemalan Mayan-Catholic deity Maximon (Saint Simon-Judas) on the candle shelf in a grocery or supermarket. The arrival of these immigrants has had another effect on hoodoo candles: While they still retain such traditional titles as **Fast Luck** and **John the Conqueror**, some have been outfitted with partial or complete Spanish translations of their names or intended manner of use.

In addition, the makers of silk screened hoodoo candles may carry a Mayan item such as the Chuparosa love candle and they might add a Santeria line with special colors and designs for the orishas or their Catholic saint equivalents.

Offertory and figure candles are dressed by rubbing them (for instance, upward to "draw" and downward to "repel") with appropriate anointing oils, such as **Fast Luck**, **Compelling**, or **John the Conqueror**. Some practitioners then sprinkle them with sachet powders or roll them in finely cut herbs selected for their specific magical powers. The time of day is also important.

To draw influences, some hoodoo practitioners say that the candle should be lit when both clock hands are rising, in the second half of the hours between six and twelve; to repel or cast off influences, they believe that the candle should be lit when both hands on the clock are falling, in the first half of the hours from twelve to six. Others prefer to light candles at midnight.

Candle Magick Divination

Candles are usually marked in some way to indicate on whose behalf they are being burned. In its simplest form, this consists of writing a petition and/or a name on paper (usually 7 or 9 times) and placing the paper beneath the candle. In addition, words or sigils may be inscribed or carved into the candle wax with a needle, pin, rusty nail, or knife, depending on the intention behind the spell.

Experienced workers often accompany the setting of lights with the burning of an appropriate incense. Some folks prefer to light the incense first to set the mood as they dress, mark, and inscribe their candles. Others believe that the lighting of the candles must come first, with the incense following.

There is also a strong contingent of spiritually-inclined folks who will not use common matches at their altars because they feel that the disposal of matches breaks the ritual flow of their movements. They prefer to light a taper in another room and bring the taper to the altar, blowing it out or snuffing it once the actual lights are set. As with all such matters, tradition and personal preferences leave room for variation.

In some spells, the candle is burned a half-inch at a time for several days. In others, it is marked into sections with pins or needles and burned a section at a time "until the pin drops." There are a number of variations of this technique that have evolved over the years. Many are distinguished by the time and location they developed. All, however, have similarities that show they originated from some central source.

In addition to burning the candle while it stands on a piece of paper, some spells specify that the candles should be moved toward or away from each other over the course of the working, or that the candle flame be used to ignite the name or petition-paper, the ashes of which are then used in the work. During the course of certain conjurations, altar candles may also be ceremonially extinguished in water or turned upside down into a saucer of graveyard dirt or even burned sideways at both end.

When a candle is burned in sections, either measured by time or by pins, it is invariably pinched out, not blown out at the end of each session, to signify that the spell is not yet complete. If pins or needles are used for measuring sections, they usually will not be discarded after they drop, but will be saved for further use.

Depending on the type of job being done, they may be used for making crosses and double crosses in the paper on which the names or desires have been written, they may be wrapped in a cloth or paper and buried or carried in a mojo hand, or they may be disposed of in a ritual manner.

Candle Magick Divination

Interpreting The Candle

Not every magical practitioner takes heed of the manner in which ritual or spell-casting candles burn, but for the most part, in my experience, it is people who work in African-American and African-Caribbean traditions who pay attention to the way a candle burns and can draw conclusions about it. In particular, spiritual workers who set lights for clients make a habit of noticing the manner in which the candles burn.

Of course, it is important to note that some candles are simply poorly made and will burn badly no matter what you do with them (for instance, if the wick is too thick they may burn sootily). Also, the temperature in the area, the presence of wind or a draft, and other external factors may play a part in how candles burn. The novice should not worry over-much about how candles burn until he or she has burned a lot of candles and gained some perspective on the matter.

All that having been said, here are some of the things to watch for when burning candles: The candle gives a clean, even burn. This means things will go well with the spell or blessing and that one will most likely get what one wishes for. If a glass encased candle burns and leaves no marks on the glass, that is best. If a free-standing candle leaves little or no residue, that is best.

A free-standing candle runs and melts a lot while burning. This gives you an opportunity to observe the flow of wax for signs. For instance, if you are burning a bride-and-groom type candle for love, and the woman's wax runs all over the man's, then the woman desires the man more than he desires her. If you are burning a green money candle and the wax melts and runs down onto the monetary offering, then the spell is "eager to work" and the candle is "blessing the money."

Some people try to influence the way melting wax runs. They do this as an intentional part of the spell-work, to increase the likelihood that things will go the way they want. Others prefer to let nature take its course and to watch running wax for signs, without interfering in its movements.

A free-standing candle burns down to a puddle of wax. When this happens, most workers will examine the shape of the wax for a sign. You may see something of importance there, for the shape may suggest an outcome regarding the matter at hand. For instance, a heart-shaped wax puddle is a good significator if you are burning a red candle for a love spell – and a coffin-shaped wax puddle is a good significator if you are burning a black devil candle against an enemy.

Candle Magick Divination

Wax puddles come in all kinds of shapes; most candle-workers treat them like tea-leaves when they read them. If a glass-encased candle burns half clean and half dirty, it indicates that there is hidden trouble with the person for whom the lights have been set or that someone is working against your wishes. Things will not go well at first, but by repeated spells you may get them to go better.

A free-standing candle lets out a lot of smoke but burns clean at the end. Again, hidden trouble or someone working against your wishes. Things will not go well at first, but with repeated work you will overcome.

There is a dirty, black, sooty burn (especially one that messes up a glass-encased candle). This means things are going to go hard -- the spell may not work, the blessing may fail, the person is in deeper stress or trouble than you thought. If the work is being done against an enemy and the enemy's candle burns sooty and dirty, then it is likely that the enemy is fighting your influences.

The candle goes out before completely burning. This is a bad sign because it indicates that someone very strong is working against you or against the person on whose behalf you are setting the lights. You will have to start the entire job over from the beginning and you may need to use stronger means than you first employed.

The candle tips over and flames up into a fire hazard. Not only will the spell probably fail, but there may be increased danger ahead for you or the client. In order to accomplish anything, you will have to start the entire job over from the beginning – but first do a thorough Uncrossing spell for everyone involved and ritually clean the premises before setting any more lights.

The candle burns up overly fast. Generally a fast burn is good, but an overly-fast burn (compared to other times you have used the same kind of candle) means that although the work will go well, it may not last long. You might have to repeat the job at a later date. If you have set lights for several people and one person's candle burns faster than the others, then that person is most affected by the work, but the influence may not last long enough to produce a permanent change.

A Simple Candle Spell: *Take one small white candle and place it in an appropriate holder. Write a wish or desire on a small piece of paper and fold in two. Light the candle with a wooden match and concentrate on what you wrote on the paper. Continue concentrating on your wish or desire and place the paper under the candle holder. Be careful that the paper does not come in contact with the flame. Sit and watch the flame while concentrating. When you feel ready, snuff out the flame. Repeat for three days.*

Candle Magick Divination

Chapter Two
Preparations With Incense And Oils

A spell, by definition, is a vehicle to access, control and direct magickal force. Candles gain access primarily by their fiery symbolism. Candle magick is a combination of the meditations above and strong visualizations to cause a specific effect, i.e. cast a spell. A "Spell" being defined as a directed release of energy set for a specific purpose. All the ritual involved serves to help focus the energy on the desired effect. It is not the candle or the flame or the "magick words" that you speak that causes the desired effect, it is the power of your mind focused towards its goal that creates the real power.

Despite what you may have read, you do not have to belong to any religion, pagan or otherwise to practice candle magick, (or any magick for that matter). However, you should always remember to use magick for positive purposes only. A good example of this rule is the *Wiccan Rede:* "An it harm none, do what ye wilt." Don't forget as well, to remember the *Rule of Three,* that everything positive or negative will be returned to you three-fold.

As in any form of magick, candle magick affects everything around you, so be very careful what you ask for, for it may just come true. The wording must not be taken lightly, be very careful, concise, and precise, and make sure you have covered all possible bases. Your mind tends to be very literal and invokes reality to take the "path of least resistance." Because of this, your wishes and desires can come true, but if you do not have a clear goal, the results may be less than pleasing for you.

Some candle magick has to be repeated over a period of days. Therefore, you will want to place them in a safe area where they will not be disturbed. A private bathroom is an ideal place, away from objects that may catch fire, and away from noises and disturbances emitted from objects such as the television and radio. Candle magick should always be performed in a low traffic area, so chose your location with care.

You need to have a flat surface to practice your magick. This is called an altar. You may use anything that has a flat top, a table, dresser, or even an inverted box with a piece of plywood on top. If you use a cover, the color can be white since this is a very versatile color. Some say this color works best with most of the spells that you will be performing. But it doesn't really matter what color you use, as long as it suits you.

Candle Magick Divination

Incense And Oils

For the beginner, the ritual of preparation for candle magick is important. As you grow more accomplished, you will develop your own personal methods to prepare. Until that time, traditional preparations are recommended to get yourself in the proper frame of mind.

Like candles, incense and oils have been used for centuries to facilitate religious, spiritual and magickal invocations. The ceremonial use of incense in contemporary ritual is most likely a relic of the time when the psychoactive properties of incense brought the ancient worshiper in touch with supernatural forces.

In the temples of the ancient world, the main sacrifice was the inhalation of incense. Incense is defined as the perfume or smoke from spices and gums when burned in celebrating religious rites or as an offering to a deity. Bronze and gold incense burners were cast very early in history and their forms were often inspired by cosmological themes representing the harmonious nature of the universe.

In the Judaic world, the vapors from burnt spices and aromatic gums were considered part of the pleasurable act of worship. In proverbs (27:9) it is said that "Ointment and perfumes rejoice the heart." Perfumes were widely used in Egyptian worship. Stone altars have been unearthed in Babylon and Palestine, which have been used for burning incense made of aromatic wood and spices.

The Egyptians, Israelites, Carthaginians, and the Arabs all developed the art and science of aromatics. For those inhabiting the fertile lands of the Nile, perfumes and incense were closely related to eternal life. The sacred bodies of the Pharaohs were mummified and covered with oils and perfume. Their fabulous burial vaults were filled with precious metals, jewels and wonderful fragrances.

This was the ritual for awaiting reincarnation, and all efforts were devoted to pleasing the gods who would soon grant immortality. The historical route of incense continued to follow the pathways of civilization.

As Greek thought and culture spread throughout the Eastern Mediterranean, so too did the use of incense. The Greeks offered incense to their gods in the hope of gaining personal favor. Throughout Greek mythology one finds many references to those perfumed essences. In the later Hellenic era, the same philosophers who discovered in the heavens the music of the spheres, found in the devoted laborious study the mystical art of perfumery.

Candle Magick Divination

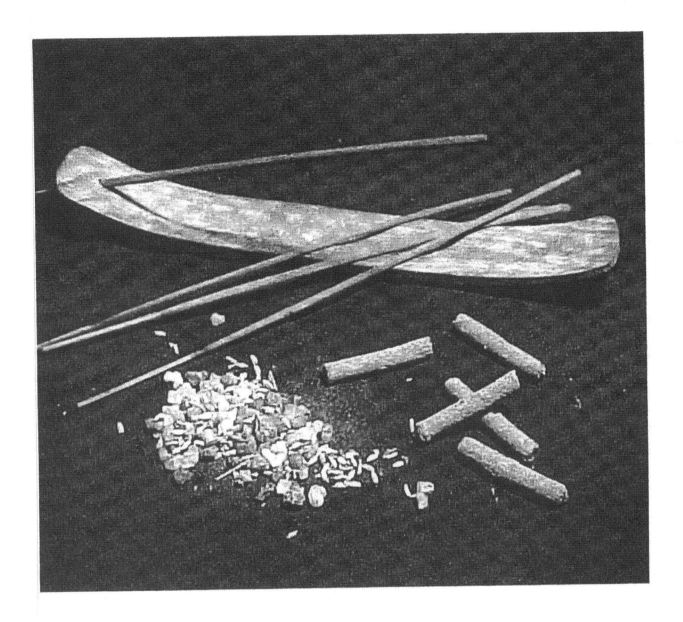

Today, most of us are familiar with the basic cone, stick, raw, or granular forms of incenses. The oldest and most original incenses have been tree resins and herbs or woods that burn with a fragrant smoke. Typical herbal incenses include sage and tobacco, which is favored by Native Americans and those who follow their traditions.

Candle Magick Divination

The Chinese discovered Musk, which is almost as popular today as it once was throughout the ancient Chinese empires. It was Chinese custom to burn incense at funerals and during burial processions, a practice that was later followed in western European culture.

By the time the Roman culture came to absorb and control the people of the ancient world, the many traditions of incense were firmly established. Along the Apia way and the sea-lanes piloted by the Roman galleys, merchants trafficked, and fortunes were made in the perfume trade.

To Tyro, Constantinople and Alexandria, the traders went out to barter for the riches of cinnamon, frankincense, and sandalwood. Military campaigns were undertaken to open up new roads to the perfumes and spices of the east and that would help fill the coffers of Rome with gold.

According to Rodale's **Illustrated Encyclopedia of Herbs**, the word perfume comes from the term for "to smoke," indicating a awareness of scent worn or carried in this way. During some historical periods, incense was used not only to purify spiritually, but purify literally as well. Herbal incenses were believed to be an important part of keeping away disease. Early doctors even recommended patients inhale incense for medicinal purposes.

Today, most of us are familiar with the basic cone, stick, raw, or granular forms of incenses. The oldest and most original incenses have been tree resins and herbs or woods that burn with a fragrant smoke. Typical herbal incenses include sage and tobacco, which is favored by Native Americans and those who follow their traditions. The best-known wood incense is the rare and expensive Sandalwood, which is made of finely shaved chips of the tree of the same name. Resin incenses, which are granular lumps of dried tree sap, include the Biblical Frankincense and Myrrh as well as Benzoin and Copal, the latter a holy incense of the Mayan Indians of Central America. Resins are often burned in mixtures, the light scent of golden Frankincense combining beautifully with richly musky Myrrh and sharply aromatic Benzoin.

Resins, especially the gummy ones, do not always light and burn well on their own, and even herbs will burn more evenly if given a start, so when burning natural incenses, it is customary to place them on burning charcoal. Special charcoal disks made for this purpose are sold by most outlets that carry resin incenses. They are lighted and put into a brazier and the incense is then placed upon them. Compounded incenses are those in which fragrances are blended into a base of very finely shaved wood.

Candle Magick Divination

Make Your Own Incense

If you so desire, you can personalize your candle magick rituals with your own homemade incense. Author Sherry Eldridge writes that: "Incense composition and use is an art form of itself." Basically, an incense is any combination of plant materials...and a base, which are mixed together and burned or smouldered on charcoal.

The possibilities are endless. They exist in virtually every plant form – root, berries, flowers, bark, resins, seeds, stems, all are good possibilities for creating an herbal incense. If you don't have an herb garden, or access to a store selling bulk herbs, the materials are still right at your fingertips, just look through your spice rack.

You'll want to make sure your incense blend includes at least one of each of the following categories:

Bases: In order for the incense to be easily ignitable and maintain a consistent burn, every mixture must have a base. Pine sawdust, cedar sawdust or powdered sandalwood are excellent bases and relatively easy to find.

Scent(s): Again, the possibilities are endless. Some good dependable items to try are rose petals, frankincense, myrrh, benzoin, copal, bay, borage, rosemary, lavender, eucalyptus, cinnamon, pine needles, juniper, dragons blood, and literally hundreds of others.

Resins: These are basically what keep your dried leaves and powders together and keep them from going "up in smoke." Some basic resins are Gum Arabic, Benzoin, Pine Needle Resin, Frankincense, Gum Mastic, Myrrh, as well as a variety of tree saps.

Just remember, while some herbs hold their fragrance, not all herbs smell the same burning as they do fresh or even dried. Some incredibly sweet herbs can burn with an acrid odor, so it's a good idea to experiment a little at first, especially before mixing an herb you aren't familiar with.

This is also a good time to mention that more does not necessarily mean better. A mixture of too many different herbs results in a combination that can be more overpowering than pleasing. With scents, as in all things, keeping it simple is often the key to success

Candle Magick Divination

If you are gathering your own ingredients, please be certain you know exactly what trees (and for that matter, all plants!) you are collecting for use. Some people choose to add a drop or two of essential oil for one of the included ingredients as a sort of binding ingredient, and while it does enhance the aroma a little, it is not absolutely necessary. Orris root is as good a scent fixative for incense as it is for potpourri, so consider adding it to your mixtures.

A mortar and pestle is usually fine for making your incense, or a grinder or food processor set to chop-to-fine. Don't put larger pieces of bark or tough stem in a food processor. Break or grind your ingredients up first. What you're looking for, depending on the plant materials, is an almost powdered consistency, leaving some slightly larger pieces which will continue to burn and last longer.

Once the consistency is right, take your nearly powdered herbal mixture and your base material and combine both with your gum or sap adhesive material. This really has to be done with mortar and pestle for a faster burning, powdery consistency, but if you don't mind a longer burning, granular consistency, the mixing can be done with something as simple as a spoon.

Some materials, such as Rose petals, may be difficult to grind if they aren't dried completely. Certain herbs, such as the Artemesias and Yarrow stem, can be difficult to grind as well, so just chop them up as small as you possibly can.

Once you have your mixture, you can use it immediately, but the incense works best when stored in an airtight container for awhile. The properties need to mix and the scents come together to create their unique blend. Be sure to label your container.

For burning, you can use those little round incense charcoals made for this specific purpose. Sprinkle a small amount of your herbal mixture on to the glowing charcoal and replenish as needed. For a cleaner burning experience, try using an incense burner, or a dish half full of salt or sand. Pile the herbal mixture on the salt/sand and light it. Replenish as needed.

A Simple Incense Spell: *Take some of your favorite incense and hold it in your hand while repeating out loud seven times: "With the smoke of this incense, my desire shall travel upwards and become energized and made real with the universe." Place your incense in its proper holder and light it with a wooden match. When the smoke begins to rise into the air, state your wish or desire into the smoke so that the rising smoke is moved about by your breath. Visualize your wish becoming one with the smoke and rising with it upwards. Repeat your wish seven times.*

Candle Magick Divination

Magickal Oils

Dressing and anointing oils have been a part of magickal practice for as far back as oral histories and written records exist. It is very likely that their use combines Native American plant lore, information derived from medieval European herbals, African traditions of healing, and "books of wonders" such as those attributed to Albertus Magnus.

Some of the occult symbolism in the old herbals is based on the so-called doctrine of signatures, whereby the shape, texture, or color of a plant is a sign of its occult uses. Other magickal ascriptions are extensions of the ways that certain herbs are used in folk medicine. Thus Violet leaves, which look like hearts, are worn in the shoe because they are alleged to attract a new lover, while Angelica root, which contains phyto-estrogens is a standard folk-remedy for women's reproductive health problems.

In mystical terminology, touching a drop of oil to your finger and then placing it on yourself or another person is called **anointing**. Drizzling oil, rubbing it, or touching a drop of it onto an inanimate object is called **dressing**. Other old synonyms for dressing are **preparing** and **fixing**.

In actual practice, most oils are used both for anointing the person and for dressing charms, candles, or mojo bags. Since many of them have very pleasant scents, they can even be treated as a form of perfume.

Essential oils are concentrated, pharmacologically active substances pressed or distilled from blossoms, leaves, bark, sap, resins, roots, and fruits of various plants and trees. It is claimed that the essence retains the magickal correspondences associated with the source from which it was taken, and therein lies the clue to using oils magickally.

Carrier oils are mild, pure oils that are used to dilute and increase the amount of oil made from the concentrated essential oils. They are used to make oil blends cost less and last longer. The most common and preferred carrier oils are Jojoba, Almond, Grapeseed, and Apricot Kernel oil. Jojoba oil is actually a liquid form of wax, and resists aging and oxidization better than any other carrier, but it is also one of the most expensive carriers. Both Almond and Apricot Kernel are high quality and relatively inexpensive. You can add crystals, stones, and herbs to oil blends to give them additional influences and energies. As long as the object will fit through the neck of the oil bottle and is non-toxic, you can add nearly anything you like.

Candle Magick Divination

You are encouraged to use caution with the use of all magickal oils. Some oils are virtually harmless, like lavender, for example. But some oils, such as lemon oil, can burn if there is exposure to the skin. Others can cause headaches, nausea. However, do not let these warnings frighten you about using the oils. Just simply use caution when necessary.

When using essential oils on the skin, with the exception of lavender and tea tree oils, always dilute with a carrier oil. A carrier oil is basically a vegetable oil that is suitable for use on the skin. Examples of these would be canola oil, almond oil, grapeseed oil, turkey red oil for bath oils, and many more.

Lavender can be applied directly to the skin, as can tea tree oil. These are the only exceptions. If you are going to use several different oils, combine them into a synergy, and use only 10 drops of that synergy. This will create the desired effect without the possibility of injury. When mixing essential oils, you will want to do so on a surface that cannot be damaged.

Some essential oils can be damaging, so cover up the area you will be working in. Spills should be cleaned up as soon as possible. The best things you can use to clean up the spill and remove the scent are vinegar, high proof vodka and grain alcohol, if it is available to you. High proof vodka or grain alcohol is good to have on hand if you will be working with essential oils. If you soak your empty bottles in it, it will remove the scent, and it is also good for cleaning.

It is important that essential oils are stored in dark glass bottles (they are usually sold in amber glass bottles) and are kept in a dark, cool place, away from light. Do not use clear glass bottles or plastic. Light will get through the clear glass, and will diminish the value and potency of the oil, and the oils will eat through plastic, or the plastic will permeate the oil, diminishing the potency and purity as well.

For convenience, you may want to have drip guards on the open mouth of your essential oil bottles. These can help reduce spills if you accidentally knock one over, and can aid in dispensing the oils drop by drop. But there are also drawbacks to the reducers.

Some oils, such as benzoin, are thick and do not easy dispense from the bottle. At these times, it is better to have a separate glass dropper for each bottle. Do not use the same dropper in multiple bottles, or you will contaminate your oils. Remember, the use of oils with your candle magick serves as an aid to energizing your consciousness. The oils themselves do not contain magick – that comes from within you.

Candle Magick Divination

Traditional Guide To Incense And Oil Fragrance

Amber - love, comfort, happiness, and healing. Amber oil is created from lesser quality amber, which is fossilized pine resin millions of years old. True amber oil is extremely rare and expensive.

Ambergris - psychic powers, dreams, aphrodisiac. This is a product of sperm whales, and was used widely for magick in the past, it is not very common today due to increased ecological considerations. Most of the ambergris oil on the market is artificial. For a close substitute, mix cypress oil with a few drops of Patchouli oil.

Apple Blossom - happiness, love, friendship.

Bayberry - protection, wishes, prosperity, happiness, control.

Benzoin - astral projection, purification.

Bergamot - money-attraction, prosperity, uplifting of spirits.

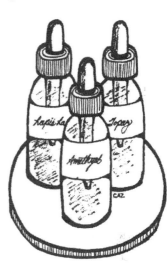

Carnation - protection, strength, healing, love, lust.

Cedarwood - healing, purification, unhexing, protection, money-attraction.

Cinnamon - purification, stimulation, wealth and prosperity, business success, lust, astral projection, healing.

Citronella - cleansing, warding off, healing, unhexing, exorcism. Don't use indoors.

Clove - pain relief, intellectual stimulation, business success, wealth and prosperity, divination, exorcism, protection, psychic awareness.

Copal - love, purification, uplifting spirits, protection, exorcism, promoting spirituality and psychic awareness.

Candle Magick Divination

Cypress - comfort, healing, and protection.

Dittany of Crete - Astral projection.

Dragon's Blood - extremely useful in adding power to any other oil, increases potency of spells and rituals, protection, courage, hex-breaking, exorcism, magickal power, love.

Eucalyptus - healing, purification, protection – open up a vial of eucalyptus oil and breathe in the vapor, or use a few drops in steam inhalation to help ease congestion with colds or allergies.

Frankincense - spirituality, astral strength, protection, consecration, courage, exorcism.

Gardenia - peace, love, healing.

Ginger - wealth & riches, invigorating, lust, love, magickal power.

Hibiscus - divination, love, lust.

Honeysuckle - money, psychic powers, happiness, friendship, healing.

Hyacinth - happiness, protection.

Jasmine - love, money, dreams, fantasy, purification, wisdom, skills, astral projection.

Juniper - calming, protection, healing, exorcism – mixed with grapefruit oil and rubbed on the body, it is said to help with cellulite – if using, pure, essential oils, remember to mix with a carrier oil such as jojoba or almond, the use of this oil can cause a skin reaction.

Lavender - cleansing, healing, love, happiness, one of the few oils that can be used undiluted on the body.

Candle Magick Divination

Lemon - healing, love, purification.

Lemongrass - psychic powers, mental clarity.

Lilac - soothing, warding off, exorcism.

Lotus - opening, elevating mood, protection, spirituality, healing, meditation. A recipe for Lotus Bouquet: Mix equal parts of Rose, Jasmine, and Musk. Then add some Ylang-Ylang to equal about 10% of the entire solution.

Magnolia - nature, trees, hair growth. A recipe for Magnolia Bouquet: Mix 2 parts Sandalwood with about 1 part Jasmine and about 1 part Rose. Add some Neroli oil to equal about 5 - 10% of the entire solution.

Musk - aphrodisiac, prosperity, inner truth, courage, purification.

Myrrh - spirituality, hex-breaking, meditation, healing, consecration, exorcism.

Neroli - confidence, insomnia.

New Mown Hay - used for new beginnings, gaining a fresh perspective on problems, or to break negative habits and thought patterns. There are several brands on the market. To make your own version, mix the following oils: Woodruff, Tonka, Lavender, Bergamot, and Oakmoss.

Oakmoss - money-drawing. To make your own oakmoss bouquet: combine vetivert and cinnamon oils.

Orange - divination, love, luck, money-attraction, psychic powers.

Patchouly - growth, love, mastery, warm & sensual.

Pennyroyal - purifying.

Candle Magick Divination

Peppermint - energy, mental stimulant, exorcism, healing.

Pine - grounding, strength, cleansing, exorcism, healing.

Rose - love, house-blessing, fertility, healing.

Rose Geranium - courage & protection.

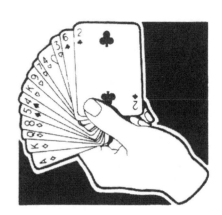

Rosemary - remembrance, energy, exorcism, healing.

Sage - wisdom, clarity, purification, exorcism.

Sandalwood - used as a general, all-purpose annointing oil. Its magickal attributes include spirituality, healing, protection, astral projection, exorcism. Cedar may be used as a substitute.

Strawberry - love, luck.

Tonka - used for love and attracting money. Mix Benzoin oil with a few drops of Vanilla extract to make a substitute.

Tuberose - for love attraction. very expensive, if you can ever find it. A substitute would contain Ylang-Ylang, Rose, and Jasmine Oils, with just a touch of Neroli added.

Vanilla - lust, mental powers.

Vetivert - unhexing, money, peace, love, exorcism.

Violet - wisdom, luck, love, protection, healing.

Yarrow - courage, exorcism, psychic.

Ylang-Ylang - Use for love, harmony, and euphoria.

Candle Magick Divination

Chapter Three
Beginning Candle Magick

Magick should reflect you and what you are doing the magick for. Keep in mind that candle magick is usually done in condensed areas so keep things as simple as you can, especially your candlesticks and censors.

Meditation is a useful tool to relax and relieve stress. It can also be used to find an answer to a difficult problem. The approaches are slightly different. You have to learn to relax before you can learn to search your inner self for answers. The answers to most of life's problems can be found within ourselves.

Sit in a quite space. Light a candle using a color of your choice. Night time is best for meditation, let the candle be the only light in the room. Empty yourself of all thought. This takes a little practice. Start by focusing on the flame, let the flame be your only thoughts. How beautiful it is, how it dances. Nothing else.

Slowly the flame will become everything, nothing else exists. This may only last a few seconds to start with. You will feel great afterwards. With practice this will last for much longer. If you can turn off the outside world for 15 or 20 minutes you are doing excellent and will feel wonderfully relaxed.

To find an answer using candles and meditation, do as above, but as the flame becomes all, lightly think about something that is troubling you. Turn it over in your mind approach it from different angles. With all other things closed out, you will find the answer.

Often times it is like a bubble that slowly drifts up from the bottom of your subconscious and pops on the surface of your conscious mind. There's your answer, it was there all the time, you just couldn't find it through the daily obstacles in your own mind.

Visualization is a key factor in this role also. For without visualization, magick cannot occur. Whenever you wish for something, you mentally place a picture of your desire in your mind. If you have ever done this, then you have visualized something. It is that simple, but it does require practice. Visualization comes easy for some and difficult for others. Because we are bombarded every second of our lives with stimuli from the outside world, it is hard for our minds to focus on any one subject more than a few seconds at a time. Proper mind control is essential to successful candle magick.

Candle Magick Divination

Choosing The Right Candle

Any type of candle can be used for candle magick as long as it has been prepared prior to use. You do not have to buy a "special" candle for your magick. But nothing says you can't as well. If it makes you happy to buy a manufactured candle that is intended for certain spells, go right ahead. You may also want to choose a candle color specific to a spell if you feel it helps your concentration.

As with any other tool, the candle made by the practitioner for a specific purpose captures the energy of the practitioner. Many experienced candle users will use only candles they have crafted themselves because of this. You should decide how often and for how long a time you are going to burn your candle. Choose your candle size according to your purpose.

If your goal is very important, you may wish to burn your candle for several days, which means you must use a large candle. An alternative, and safer method, is to use several smaller candles and burn one each day.

Preparing Your Area

You are now ready to prepare your quiet room for candle magick. Close your eyes and relax. Visualize using your hands to sweep out all the negativity from your room. Physically use your hands in a sweeping motion while pushing all the gray negativity out the door. See it seeping from every nook and cranny in your area, and out the door. Imagine compressing all the negativity into a small black ball, then let it out into the universe.

Next, visualize while using your hands in an opening and closing manner, that you are illuminating every inch of your room. Light every part of your area, making sure not to miss any corners, nooks and crannies. See in your mind the entire room lit up as if a thousand lights were beaming down from the sky and up from the earth. Concentrate on this light seeking out the last bits of darkness anywhere negativity may try and hide, and blasting it apart with the pure white light of universal truth and consciousness.

If you feel you have not gone over it thoroughly enough, do it again. Soon your room should be pulsating with white light. Feel it surround and envelop you. Open your eyes and say aloud: ***All ill and negativity has been banished and positive vibes instilled. I say it is so!*** Your area is now ready.

Candle Magick Divination

Candle Annointing

Annoint your candle with the oil that you have chosen. This is done by placing a little of the oil on your fingertips. Grasp the candle at its midpoint with your left index finger and thumb, and use your right index finger and thumb to stroke oil on the candle from the midpoint up to the top of the candle.

Next, grasp the candle at its midpoint with your right index finger and thumb, and use your left index finger and thumb to stroke oil on the candle from the midpoint down to the bottom of the candle. Continue in this fashion until the entire candle has been annointed. This is also known by some as "dressing the candle."

Some practitioners of candle magick, if they are wanting to bring something to them, will rub the oil in a downward motion from the top to the middle, and then from the bottom to the middle. To send something away from you, rub the oil from the middle of the candles out to the ends.

If working with a glass-enclosed candle, oil the exposed wax clockwise to draw good, counter-clockwise to expel negativity.

While ritually annointing your candle, visualize a pure white beam of light coming up from the ground, entering your body through the soles of your feet and another beam of white light coming down from the universe and entering your body through the top of your head.

Envision the energy of these beams of light flowing throughout your body and mingling together, finally concentrating in your hands, causing them to feel warm and to tingle. Now continue to stroke your candle until you feel the energy from your hands transfer to the candle. Your candle is now charged with your personal energy.

Inscribing the Candle

Scratching words or symbols is a popular way to focus your thoughts when using candle magick. Take a sharp object, such as a pin, and carve appropriate words and/or symbols into the side (or top if it's glass-enclosed) of the candle. If working for prosperity, a dollar sign may be appropriate. If the goal is romance, a heart would work. Astrological signs, runes, element signs, or personal signs may also be used. The same principle as dressing a candle should be used. To draw something to you, write from the top to the middle then from the bottom to the middle. To repel things, write

Candle Magick Divination

Scratching words or symbols is a popular way to focus your thoughts when using candle magick. Symbols should have a personal significance to use them effectively. Marked candles should be properly disposed of after use.

Candle Magick Divination

from the middle to the ends. Visualize your goal while you carve, or speak out loud several times what you want to accomplish. The key is to implant, firmly in your mind, what it is you want to achieve.

Each candle should be used for one purpose only. If you prepare a candle for prosperity purposes, don't use it for anything else. If you use several candles, remember to prepare each one before use.

Know Your Goals

When performing candle magick you should consider the steps one must take to ensure the desired result. First you must define the goal you wish to reach. Be very explicit and clear as to this desire.

One good method is to keep a magickal journal to write down the goal(s)/desire(s) you wish to achieve. In this journal, you need to clarified exactly what it is you desire and how you are to obtain it. You must be very careful in this. Remember the old saying: ***Be careful what you wish for, you may just get it?*** That epitomizes the caution which you must exercise in defining your goals.

Don't take magickal goals lightly. As with everything in life there is cause and effect. Any thing you do has an effect on everything else.

In developing your goal, it will come as a desire/wish. Take this and dissect it. Write this out. Look at it from every conceivable angle. Question every word. Does it feel right? Will it harm you? Will it harm anyone? Should it say "we" instead of "I" ? Is it imposing on another?

Ask yourself: "Why am I asking for this goal?" Have you done all you could to manifest it as so? Are you relying too heavily on this? Is it reasonable? Do you need to change the wording? Have you thought this out completely? Are you truly sure of this wish?

Now have you have thought it out, visualized the way in which you wish it to manifest, what about the result? Have you truly thought of all the ramifications? What will happen when you get your desire? How will it affect you? Others? What if it comes and you find yourself unhappy? What would you do if this makes someone else unhappy. Remember, everything you do will have an effect. If you are casting a love spell, will this spell have bad consequences on anyone else?

Candle Magick Divination

A Magickal State Of Mind

You now need to prepare yourself for magick. Your state of mind is of utmost importance in any magickal endeavor. You must take great care in drawing energies upon yourself, which will be released by your concentration as a thought form when you light your candle. This thought form has reality, so take care.

You will need to know how to harness, work within, and then release the tremendous amount of energy you will be dealing with. Fire is one, if not the strongest and most potent forms of the elements. Thought forms associated with fire can be powerful when working candle magick, and you must learn how to control them, otherwise things can really go wrong and you may find yourself in a worse situation then before you started.

Now you are ready to cast your first spell. In your chosen area, light the candle and picture your need. As we have said before, there is no need to invoke ancient deities. (You can if you want.) All you really need is to believe that lighting the candle will help. Visualize your need. If you are needing more money, then visualize all of your bills paid, money for new school clothes for the kids. Don't focus on how the money will come, just that it will. Picture the bills paid, see the children in their new clothes.

Meditate on your need and let the candle burn, do not leave unattended candles burning. It is alright to put a candle out and light it again later. (Don't blow your candle out, snuff it.) Every time you re-light it, picture your need. Burn it until it is gone. What you need will come to you if the energies permit.

Don't despair if it seems the magick has not worked for you. Perform the candle magick for three days in a row, and then wait three weeks. Then try again for three more days. Be patient, it is amazing sometimes how the universe in concert with your own inner consciousness will provide for you. You may not get exactly what you wanted. But a majority of the time, most will say that they were satisfied by the outcome.

After performing your candle magick spell, be extra watchful for coincidences that could have meaning to the wish or desire expressed with your spell. This kind of coincidence is called *synchronicity*, or "meaningful coincidence." Often, the results of candle magick will manifest itself as synchronicity. Because of this, people often ignore or dismiss this meaningful event, and miss the life path being set in front of them. Magick works within the laws of the universe.

Chapter Four
The Many Forms Of Divination

Candle magick is popular not only because it is simple to get started with, but because it is complete within itself. When doing candle magick, one needs little more than the candle to do the entire working. One little known aspect of candle magick is the ability to channel ones psychic energies in order to see the future. This is called: **Divination**, or by its popular name, fortune telling.

Divination is the art of seeing into the possible future using any one of several methods to obtain information which is not directly accessible to the conscious mind. There are many different kinds of divination, Whether you use cards, crystals, a pendulum, ink, lead, dice, the flight of birds or anything else, what you are really doing is opening your end of a channel to higher wisdom.

Each person will find that certain forms of divination work best for them, while others do not. It all stems from how open you are to the future. You have to be very careful not to see what you want to see, but to see the true possibilities that confront us all.

The future is not set in stone. It is merely shadows of what can be if we continue on our current life path. The future moves and flows like a body of water. Nearly everything you see can be changed if you want it so. Your actions are what determine your future. This is why looking into the far future is a chancy and a rather unreliable prospect.

Divination is an art. Secondly it is an action. Working both together, it is a system of obtaining hidden or unknown insights or guidance into the subtle energies of the movements, patterns and paths in one's life.

Perhaps second only to the discipline of the mind through meditation, the art of divination is the system by which many of our basic desires can be guided to success.

No matter what tool you use, the basics are that they are used to aid the reader to tune into the mind's ability to read the subtle energies that permeate our existence. It is a language of symbols, a vehicle in which the reader can interpret the energies he or she is exchanging and engaging in at a particular time.

Once you have chosen your own method of divination, you must work with this and become completely comfortable with it. Trying to use divination without a thorough

Candle Magick Divination

knowledge of its concepts, symbols and certain languages will lead to frustration. As you are working with your method of choice, you will begin to notice an increase in your awareness. The more you work with this, the more you will learn to trust your own hunches, intuition, precognition.

One of the hardest things to deal with in working with divinatory tools is framing your question. Learning how to ask a question is as important as translating it. Try to narrow down the question, focus in on what it is you need to know and give the tool the means by which to answer you.

Given time and familiarity with the method you have chosen, you will instinctively know what it is you have asked and the message you have received. Much like candle magick, think about the question, write it down, phrase it as such that it will give the tool a path in which it can answer you.

Remember that sometimes you will get confusing answers to your questions. This may indicate that this is not the right time to answer your questions. Wait a week and try again when the situation has had time to evolve. As you work with it, it will come to you.

Divination is not a "right answer" kind of practice. If you ask a candle: "Should I marry this person?" You will not get advice about whether to marry or not. You will get insight into the strengths and weaknesses of that union.

You will get an exploration of the issues which that potential marriage raises for you. It can be like a good therapy session – through dialogue and exploration of these issues you can arrive at your own truest desire and choices.

When someone else is interpreting the future for you, they should be a facilitator for this process. If they say: "Yes you should marry," or "No you should not marry this person, because..." they are not using the tool the way it should be used. They are interjecting their own choices, preferences and decisions.

No single element of your method of divination is "bad" or "negative" in and of itself. It tells you something about energy, about the relations of one theme to another in your life, and it is always up to you to determine the value of this information for yourself.

If you ask someone, "did you go to the show last night?" You are likely to get a "yes" or "no" in response. If you ask: "What did you do last night?" You are likely to get a brief phrase: "Went to a show." If, however, you ask an open-ended question, such as "tell me about your evening," you are less likely to limit or shape the response.

Candle Magick Divination

Asking The Proper Questions

There is an art to asking good questions in divination. The question you pose can tell you a lot about your own stance or approach to an issue. If you find yourself saying, "Should I do such and such," you can hear your own desire to be told what to do, your own fear and uncertainty.

If you say, "Give me some insight into this question," or "what would be most productive to focus on." This way, you are creating an opportunity for real dialogue with your inner self and the universe.

In the values of many choices, there is no single right choice, right stance, right answer available, for there is only the awareness of what each choice will yield, what each choice means emotionally and symbolically to you. How each choice challenges or creates blockage for you.

The practice of divination is not a matter of checking in with the universe to see if you are living your life correctly, or to ask where your life will lead. It is a matter of gaining insight into the themes and movements of energy which you are participating in at any given time.

The interpretation that emerges from a reading is just a chance to exercise and test out your intuition and precognition. Given the seeds you are planting, what is the garden likely to yield?

If you, or another reader, see prediction in the divination session, it is not a sentence passed upon you. The future is not predetermined. Your life is subject to the rules of the universe and the infinite choices you can take. You may have some soul appointments that you have made on the inner level, but ultimately you have free will in your actions and events.

True divination doesn't answer questions, it responds. Sometimes it says: "Pay attention to these factors." Sometimes it says: "The real issue or question is this." Sometimes it says: "Here is an aspect you haven't considered." Sometimes the answer is completely unclear at the time you are asking.

You see the shapes in the candles flame, or the way the smoke curls upwards, but they just don't yield clear information. Then the message is: "Wait. It is not time to know." Your question has been posed, and your inner self will find other modes and experiences for you, which will guide you to understanding and proper insight over time.

Candle Magick Divination

The more you work with a divination tool, the more you will develop an instinct for whether it is addressing your question, or whether it is showing you how to re-frame the question or issue. In the process of doing regular readings for yourself, you get to clarify your priorities. You get to see which questions yield the greatest insights, and learn more about your own way of perceiving information.

We tend to focus on divination more as an activity that you do with yourself and for yourself. Yet many go to others for readings or feel tempted to do readings for friends and family. The value of having someone else read for you is that they can provide openings or insights for you that activate your ability to do it for yourself.

If a reader tells you that the theme of the next year for you is finding family, and that fits with your sense of need and inner truth, then hearing the reader formulate it reminds you of what you already know. It helps you to recognize your own inner truth. But if it does not ring a bell, and just seems like a foreign concept, you will probably ignore it, or decide that they are not very good at what they are doing. You may feel upset and wonder what is wrong with you.

The point of going to another person for guidance is not to see whether they are right or wrong, but rather to get information you can use for your own growth. If the other person puts you in touch with your own inner truth, then they are being helpful. If the person stirs up doubts that don't lead to positive growth and understanding, then they are not being helpful.

The same is true for you, if you choose to do readings for others. You would probably not go out after spending a few months learning a new language, and try to counsel others in that new language, because you would be too self-conscious of your limitations, and of the nuances you would be missing. So as you wish to introduce your divination games to others, it is healthy to keep it as a form of play, rather than taking on the stance of counselor or adviser.

The following pages list some of the methods which humans have developed to determine the future. This list has been gathered from all over the world and from all times. The multitude of different methods of divination demonstrate that we have always desired to know what lies ahead.

Many of these divinations remain mysterious and unknown. The exact techniques involved in the use of salt, for example, have been lost. For others, conflicting information exists as to the proper use of the tools and the methods of interpreting the messages that they produce.

Candle Magick Divination

Methods Of Divination

AEROMANCY - Divination by specific and deliberate observation of atmospheric phenomena, including clouds, storms, comets, winds and other forces.

AILECTRYOMANCY - Divination with roosters. Outdoors, a circle was created of small pieces of paper, each of which bore one of the letters of the alphabet. One kernel of dried corn was put on each of these letters. A white rooster was then placed in the center of the circle. The letters from which the rooster pecked the grain spelled out a message that pertained to the diviner's future. A most ancient form of divination and an aspect of ornithomancy.

ALEUROMANCY - Divination practiced with flour. Words and sentences stating possible futures were written on small slips of paper. Each piece of paper was rolled up in a ball of flour. The balls were then mixed thoroughly nine times and one was chosen. The chosen ball, when read, revealed the future. Apollo presided over this form of divination. The fortune cookie is a modern form of this ancient practice.

ALOMANCY - Salt as a tool of divination. Very little is known about this ancient method. Perhaps it was related to sand reading.

ALPHITOMANCY - The use of wheat or barley in an oracular trial, the purpose of which was to discover which person was guilty of some crime. The suspects were rounded up, Each was required to say, "If I am deceiving you, may this bread act upon me foul." A portion of barley or wheat bread was then served to each suspect. Those innocent of the crime would suffer no ill effects, while the guilty party would experience an attack of indigestion so painful that it was impossible to conceal it.

AMNIOMANCY - Divination by examination of the caul that occasionally covers a child's face or head at birth. This revealed the child's future life.

ASTRAGALOMANCY - A letter, word or symbol was written on each of a dozen knuckle-bones. The bones (ancient precursors to dice) were thrown on the ground and the future was determined by their positions and by the symbols that lay face up.

Candle Magick Divination

AUSTROMANCY - Divination from the winds.

AXINOMANCY - Divination by means of an axe. Two methods were in common use. In the first, an axe was tossed into the air in an open area free of trees. If tossed correctly, its blade would stick into the ground. Prognostications were made from the direction in which the axe handle pointed and the amount of time that it remained standing before falling to the ground. A second method is closely related to the first, but was only used to discover the presence of buried treasure. An axe handle was heated in a fire until red hot. The axe was placed on the ground in the area where treasure may exist in such a way that the axe's sharp edge faced the sky. A round agate was then placed on the edge. If it remained there without moving, no treasure was in the area. If it fell, it would roll quickly away. This ritual was repeated two more times. If the agate rolled toward the same direction all three times, that was the most ideal place to dig, for the treasure was within thirty-one paces. If it rolled in a different direction each time, more searching was required. Axe divination was also used in some cultures to determine the most auspicious place for a woman to give birth.

BELOMANCY - Prognostications from arrows. A popular form of divination throughout the world, especially in Greece, Rome and the Middle East. There are at least two methods: An arrow was shot into the sky straight up. The direction of the arrow's flight, and the position in which it landed, revealed the future. A second method consisted of shooting arrows at a rock and interpreting the markings the arrowheads made against its surface. This practice existed among the Greeks, and still later among the Arabians.

BIBLIOMANCY - A book was opened at random and the text revealed the future. Alternately, a pin was pushed into a book while closed; then the book was opened, and the relevant passage read. Any type of book was used, but many Christians use the Bible for this quite non-Christian practice. In ancient Greece, the works of Homer were preferred, as were those of Euripides. The Romans relied on Virgil. A variant on this practice is as follows: ask a yes or no question. Open a book at random, close your eyes and bring your finger down onto a sentence. Count of the number of letters within the sentence, ignoring punctuation. If there are an even number of letters, the answer is yes. If odd, no.

Candle Magick Divination

BOTANOMANCY - Divination with plants.

CAPNOMANCY - Divination by smoke.

CATOPTROMANCY - Divination through the use of mirrors.

CARTOMANCY - Divination through the use of regular playing cards or the Tarot.

CAUSMOMANCY - Divination by fire.

CEPHALOMANCY - An ancient form of divination performed using a donkey's skull.

CERAUNOSCOPY - Divination performed by observation of the wind – its strength, direction, or absence. Whirlwinds were also observed.

CEROSCOPY - Divination with molten wax. The wax is melted in a brass pot over a low fire and is then slowly poured into a vessel filled with cold water. The symbols and shapes created as the wax hardens in the water are read for omens of the future.

CHEIROMANCY - (also known as palmistry) Divination by studying the marks and lines of the hand, as well as their shapes, and the condition of the fingernails, to determine a person's future and character.

CLEIDOMANCY - Divination through the use of a key suspended from a thread and held between the thumb and forefinger. The key was lowered into a glass and a question asked. The key would knock upon the glass; one knock meant yes, two no. Similar to dactylomancy.

CLEROMANCY - The casting of lots; also, divination through the use of dice.

COSCINOMANCY - Divination with a sieve and tongs or shears. An old method of discovering the identity of a person responsible for a crime.

Candle Magick Divination

CRITOMANCY - Divination by food. Usually associated in ancient times with the food left or burnt on altars for offerings, especially cakes, which were a preferred sacrifice. A modern form consists of baking small objects (thimbles, whole walnuts, rings and so on) into cakes or pancakes, or inserting them into mashed potatoes. The person who is served the piece containing the charm determines her or his future according to its traditional meaning. Rings mean marriage; walnuts, health; silver coin, money. This practice dates back to at least 1778 in England.

CROMNIOMANCY - Divination with onions.

CRYSTALLOMANCY - Divination through the use of a sphere of quartz crystal.

CYCLOMANCY - Divination through the consultation of a turning wheel; probably the forerunner of the famous gambling tool, the wheel of fortune.

DACTYLOMANCY - Divination with rings.

DAPHNOMANCY - Divination with laurel (bay) leaves or branches.

DENDROMANCY - Divination through the use of oak and mistletoe.

ELAEOLANCY - A form of water gazing in which a liquid surface is studied to present the future.

EXTISPICY - Divination by observation of the entrails of sacrificed animals. This ancient art has long died out in most cultures.

GEOMANCY - Divination by the swelling, noises and movement of the earth. Also, studying cracks made in dried mud by the sun. Later, an elaborate form was created, using dots made at random to determine the future.

GYROMANCY - A curious form of divination in which several persons whirled around in circles within a large ring, the perimeter of which was marked with the letters

Candle Magick Divination

of the alphabet. As the dancers became dizzy, they would occasionally step upon one or more of the letters, and it was from the words thus formed that the future was divined.

HEPATOSCOPY - Divination by examination of the liver of a sacrificed animal. Practiced in ancient Greece, Rome, Babylon and elsewhere in the ancient world.

HIPPOMANCY - Divination with horses. The ancient Celts kept special white horses in sacred groves of trees. During sacred processions, the horses followed the lead cart, and the future was divined by their behavior. A second method was in use by the ancient Germans, who kept sacred horses in some of their temples. If, while leaving the temple to carry warriors into battle, the horse's left forefoot was the first to step outside the holy precincts, the warriors were convinced that they would not be successful, and so canceled the planned surprise attack.

HYDROMANCY - Divination by water.

LAMPADOMANCY - Omens of the future obtained by observation of the flickering of torches. If the torch's flame formed itself into one point, the signs were favorable; into two points, unfavorable, while three points on the same torch was considered the most auspicious of all. If the flame bent, the healthy would become sick in a short amount of time; if the torch was suddenly extinguished for no apparent reason, disaster was in the offing.

LECANOMANCY - The observation of oil dropped onto water.

LIBANOMANCY - The observation of smoke rising from incense.

LITHOMANCY - This form of divination used polished (not faceted) stones to create predictions of the future. Little is known about this ancient art, but it's likely that large, gleaming stones could have been used in the same manner as was the crystal ball. A specific type of stone, described as being black and finely veined with another mineral, was held to the eyes and the future divined by reading the lines on the stone's surface.

Candle Magick Divination

LYCHNOMANCY - In ancient times, divination from the flame of an oil lamp. Today, another name for divination with candles.

MARGARITOMANCY - Divination with pearls.

METOSCOPY - Character divination by the observation of a person's forehead.

MOLYBDOMANCY - Divination with lead. A small quantity of the heavy metal was melted and poured quickly into a bowl of water. The future was read in the shapes thus created. (A similar method consisted of pouring the molten lead onto the ground and, after it had cooled, observing its forms.) This form of divination can produce the most unusual shapes, perfect for symbolism.

MYOMANCY - A curious form in which the squeaks of mice, together with the damage that they cause, are interpreted as omens of the future.

NEPHELOMANCY - Divination from the appearance of clouds.

NUMEROLOGY - Character divination through the study of numbers.

OINOMANCY - (also oenomancy) Gazing into a goblet filled with dark red wine.

OLOLYGMANCY - Predictions based on the howling of dogs. These are usually considered to be negative omens.

ONEIROMANCY - The interpretation of dreams. This was once highly favored, as dreams, when requested, were believed to have been sent by the deities.

ONOMANCY - Divination based on names. Related to numerology.

ONYCHOMANCY - Divination by gazing at highly polished fingernails, onychomancy was usually performed outdoors in full sunshine. The preferred owner of the fingernails was a young boy who was still a virgin.

Candle Magick Divination

OOMANTIA - Divination through the inspection of egg whites.

ORNITHOMANCY - Divination through the observation of birds.

PEGOMANCY - Divination by the sounds, murmurings and appearance of water flowing from a fountain.

PESSOMANCY - Divination with pebbles.

PLASTROMANCY - Divination through the use of turtles' shells.

PHYLLORHODOMANCY - Divination by rose leaves.

PHYSIOGNOMY - Character divination from the appearance of the human body, including the forehead, the position of moles, facial types and so on.

PYROMANCY - Divination by fire.

RHABDOMANCY - The use of specially prepared branches or magic wands to uncover hidden treasures (gold, oil, water, etc.). Pliny wrote that it was in use by the forerunners of the Romans, the Etruscans, to find hidden sources of water. By the fifteenth century this practice had been imported from Germany to England. It has always been used in China. The modern form is known as dowsing or water witching.

RHAPSODOMANCY - A form of oracle wherein a book of poetry is opened at random and the passage that immediately reveals itself before the eyes is searched for divinatory clues. Another name for bibliomancy.

SCYPHOMANCY - Divination with the use of cups or vases.

SIDEROMANCY - Divination from the burning of straws.

SPODOMANCY - Divination through the use of ashes.

Candle Magick Divination

STOLISOMANCY - Divination from the observance of the act of dressing.

SYCOMANCY - Divination with leaves, often those of fig trees.

TASSEOGRAPHY - Divination by the observation of tea leaves left in the bottom of a cup that has been drunk. The wet tea leaves clinging to the sides of a cup are read with symbolic thought. This can be a highly effective method of divination.

TEPHRAMANCY - Use of wind or breath in divination.

TIROMANCY - (also known as tyromancy) A curious form of divination involving cheese. It may have consisted of observing milk as it curdled. The curds so formed might have been interpreted with symbolic thought. A modern form of tiromancy was recorded by a folklore specialist in Cleveland in 1960. On New Year's Eve, cut a thick slice from a wheel of Swiss cheese. Study the holes in it on one side only. If there are an odd number, the coming year will be unfavorable. If an even number, favorable. Additionally, a preponderance of small holes means minor luck or pains, while a greater number of large holes indicates major events.

XYLOMANCY - Divination with wood. A question was asked while walking in the forest. The ground was watched. Any pieces of wood found lying there were interpreted according to their shape, type (if known), and so on.

There are four classic methods of divination using candles: *Pyromancy* or *Pyroscopy* is divination by fire. *Capnomancy* is divination by smoke. *Ceromancy* is divination by molten wax dropped into water. And the art of divination using a candle is called: *Lampadomancy*.

One favorite divining method developed by Dragonstar is to take three candles of different colors: one red, the other green and the third white. Assign each candle a desire or wish that you would like to see happen. For instance, the red candle could be for finding true love. The green candle could be for financial success. While the white candle could be for better health. Light all three candles while saying out loud your desires. Allow the candles to burn for seven minutes. Now, with one breath, try to blow all three candles out at once. Those that remain lit will come true.

Chapter Five
Candle Divination

A candle is made up of different elements and different parts which represent different things. The candle itself contains the elements of Water, Air and Earth. When lit, the elements of Fire and the Spirit are employed. So a lit candle incorporates all of the classical elements, making it an extremely effective magickal tool.

Down throughout history you will find numerous references to the use of candles in many of our modern day activities. Fire was the ultimate tool used for banishing and cleansing, destruction and worship, life and death.

The body of the candle can be made from a variety of ingredients, from tallow to beeswax, it can include herbs, scents or even gems and stones. The body consists of the top half which starts at the wick down to the center. The bottom half is from the base up to the center.

In performing candle magick you are adding the necessary element of your will, or desire. The wick represents the human potential. A candle needs a wick to be lit, a wick needs a human to light it. When lit, we are sending off our human desires in hopes of manifestation and completion.

The noises you hear from the burning candle or the wax shapes it leaves can help you in communicating with your candle, speaking or acknowledgment of your wish. The candle speaking happens especially in times when figure candles are used such as the Male or Female, Skull, Cat, or any number of symbolic figures you may use to enhance your will and desire.

The shape of the burned wax when left to flow on its own can also be very revealing. Check back and see if the candle left you a message in the shape of the burned wax. You will have to take into consideration your own special circumstances and situation when interpreting the flows and shapes of melted candle wax.

Remember that each candle is as different as our own personal wish. You should learn the different ways in which a candle will speak to you. An example, if your desire is to draw a new love, you might get a very soft and muted pop or snap sound. This is the candle whispering your thoughts and desires for the forces to take hold. If, however, you are hiding something, holding back or in some way have a negative thought, you might hear some strong snaps, cracks and popping.

Candle Magick Divination

This is the candle's way of letting you know that it is fighting against the negative thoughts and forces. If the sound is in between, not quite so soft and not quite so loud, it may be trying to tell you something. Stop for a minute and let it speak to you.

You may be surprised if you suddenly have a new idea or learn that everything will be okay and a peaceful feeling comes over you. Learn to listen to the candle.

The flame, or halo, of the candle is the life of the fire itself. Upon lighting the wick, we have now included the elements of Fire and Spirit along with the human will into the candle. It can speak to us if we are watchful and aware. We can learn how it can acknowledge our wishes. It casts a halo or aura outside of itself and is usually regarded as the state of the highest potential of Spirit. The resultant smoke is what carries our prayers and wishes out to the forces, thus creating our simple act of magick.

Watching the actions of the flame, you will also see the candle speaking. Again, no two candles are going to react the same way. Use your imagination and think about what it is you have asked of the candle and apply it to the actions. Pay close attention to what you see and hear. You will soon learn automatically to recognize what the candle has to say.

Each tiny movement of the flame will tell us something. This is the life of the element of Fire and it has the ability to communicate with us, if we are only willing to listen to what it has to say.

A strong tall flame will tell us that the energy we are using is indeed inherent in the candle and it is empowered by our desire or will. This is an excellent sign of acknowledgment by the candle.

A leaping or jumping flame can indicate indecisiveness on your part. Make sure you are clear before you begin. It can also indicate that instability in emotions or actions are the problem and need to be worked on.

A weak or small flame may mean there are just too many negative energies at this time and you may have to repeat the process again at a later time. It could also indicate a communication problem, a smothering of emotions, or the inability to make a decision one way or another.

The direction of the smoke from the flame can tell us a lot. If the smoke goes to the north, this can indicate that true manifestation will be revealed, a physical happening is occurring. Physical labor can be indicated or a need for stability. If it concerns a health question, you may want a second opinion and pay closer attention to your health. Or it may even mean that a check up is indicated. Finances need to be scrutinized.

Candle Magick Divination

If the smoke heads south, this is an excellent sign. If your question concerns health, a recovery will be imminent. If it concerns love, a passionate love affair is on its way shortly. If it concerns the home, you will find new ideas and the energy to expedite these. If concerned about work, success is on its way.

You must be careful with this as it all sounds almost too good to be true. You must remember, fire can burn if you get too close, so keep your head on your shoulders and watch out for the unexpected.

If the smoke flows east there will be some mental as opposed to physical labor involved. The candle is telling you to sit and follow your head in this situation. Practice logic and patience. Think before you speak. A waiting period. No rash decisions. If applied correctly, success will be yours.

If your smoke flows to the west, you have emotions literally flooding everywhere. It could indicate a period of intense emotions in whatever your desire is. A warning of excess could be indicated. You could be too close to the situation and need to back off it for awhile. Or it could indicate that you need to clarify this thing more.

Ground yourself. Clear off the emotional aspect of it and look more towards the rational part. Each candle and wish is different, learn to apply it to the present wish.

You must remember the desire when interpreting these signs and apply them to the situation. Sometimes you may not get the message that you expect. Learn to incorporate all of the signs you are given. Separate them when searching them out and then learn how they all interact together. You may get a completely different answer when applied to another of the signs.

Step back and do some more thinking. Did you clear and calm yourself first? Have you got some leftover emotions hanging around? Are you willing the candle? Is your attention totally focused? Are you truly being honest with yourself? These and many other things must be considered when communicating with your candle.

To some, the idea of getting instructions concerning the future, desires, magick spells, etc. from a candle and its flame, can seem almost ludicrous. Some candle diviners may even consider the flame to be alive in some sense, and thus able exhibit an intelligence of some sort. This intelligence, with its connections with the mystical fire is what some think is the source of the needed information.

It doesn't matter what you believe. What does matter is that you do believe. As time passes our belief systems change and evolve. What may have made perfect sense in the past, may now seem outdated. Just trust that the process does work.

Candle Magick Divination

Candle Colors For Divination

Though white candles can be used for divination, you may wish to choose a candle whose color matches the nature of your question, as listed below:

White: All questions.

Black: Changes in luck - either good or bad, unexpected happenings, doubts, depression.

Purple: Position, authority.

Blue: Sickness, health and recovery.

Green: Family, children, births, money, jobs.

Yellow: Relocation for work, moving in general, passing tests, communication (upcoming meetings, letters, phone calls), theories.

Orange: Physical actions and activity of all kinds.

Red: Love, relationships.

Pink: Friendships.

Candle Magick Divination

Divination Using Candles

This is a method using just one candle and is an excellent way for the novice to try out this wonderful form of divination. It is so easy that anyone can try it out for the first time and achieve successful results.

Simply light one candle with a wooden match. Keep your candle lit for several hours, with no drafts nearby. Ask a yes or no question. Now sit quietly and watch the candle for any changes.

If the right side burns faster than the left, the answer is YES. If the reverse, the answer is NO. When burning a candle to determine future influences on a given subject, the right signifies good fortune. However, if the left side burns more quickly than the right, prospects do not look favorable.

Three Candles

This is a simple form of divination using three candles: Set up three candles in a triangle, making sure all candles are the same size. With this spell the color of the candles does not matter.

Close all doors and windows to make sure the room is free of drafts. Turn out the lights, then light all three candles with the same match. Speak aloud directly at the candle your question or wish. Repeat this three times. Sit and watch the flame while visualizing your question.

❑ If one candle burns more brightly than the other it means success and good fortune.

❑ If the end of any of the three wicks displays a bright shining point it is a lucky omen.

❑ If a flame moves from side to side it indicates that you will soon travel.

Candle Magick Divination

❑　If there are sparks rising from a candle you need be cautious.

❑　If the flame of one candle seems to twist and spiral it means that your enemies are plotting against you.

❑　If a flame rises and falls it suggest there is danger approaching.

❑　If one of the candles goes out suddenly without good reason it warns of great disaster.

A Multi-Candle Divination

Set up as many identical candles in holders as you have choices facing you. If you wish an answer to a simple question, two candles: one for yes, one for no. In an area free of breezes, name each candle for one of your choices individually and light them. The first to burn down and sputter out, candle YES, or candle NO, is your answer.

Using A White Candle At Night

This is a way to do candle divination using only one white candle. This method is best done in the quiet of the night, and with the lights lowered for a more intimate atmosphere. Light a candle and place it in its holder. Sit or stand before it and search for signs from the flame itself and its wick.

❑　If the flame seems dim, it may be best to hold off on plans for the time being. An extremely bright flame is a sign of good fortune, but if the flame quickly grows smaller, the luck will only be temporary.

Candle Magick Divination

Watching the actions of the flame, you will see the candle speaking. No two candles are going to react the same way. Use your imagination and think about what it is you have asked of the candle and apply it to the actions.

Candle Magick Divination

❑   If the flame waves about, bad weather may be coming, or a great change in circumstances is foretold. A spark visible in the wick indicates the imminent arrival of good news. If the flame turns in a circle or seems to form a spiral, danger is forecast. A halo around the flame indicates an approaching storm.

Watching The Wax Drip

Another age-old way of reading candles involves watching the manner in which the molten wax drips down the candle sides. Place the candle in a holder. Ask a yes or no question while lighting the wick.

Watch it for some time. If the wax drips only on the left side, the answer is no. If on the right, yes. If equally on both sides, no response is possible. If no wax drips down, ask again later.

You can also light a candle, focus on your question and drip the melted wax into a dish or pan of water, then interpret the symbols/shapes the wax makes as it hardens. We will discuss this method further in a later chapter.

Lemons And Candles

A rather unusual form of candle divination involves the use of fresh lemon juice. Obtain a clean, non-ball point or felt-tip pen. You can also use a small, sharpened stick made of clean wood.

Squeeze the juice from one lemon into a small bowl. Lay three, five or seven pieces of paper on a flat surface.

Dipping the pen into the lemon juice, write a possible outcome on each piece of paper with the juice; the juice here acts as the ink. Since lemon juice is invisible and difficult to write with, reduce these future possibilities to just a few words. Remember, simplicity is often the best route for a clear answer. Write what you think could happen in your future, both good and bad. Be honest with yourself. What would you like to happen? What do you expect to happen? Allow the papers to completely dry.

Candle Magick Divination

Light a candle. Place the slips of paper into a bowl. Mix them with your left hand, then choose one at random. Hold the chosen piece of paper close enough to the flame to heat it but not enough to burn it. The heat will reveal the contents written on the paper as the lemon juice darkens. This will determine your possible future. This method has been traced back to at least biblical times when secret societies would write hidden messages on parchment for those with the knowledge to read.

Four Candles Set In A Triangle

Write your question on a small, white piece of paper. Light four candles all of the same color and place three of them in a triangle with the remaining candle set in the middle next to or on top of the paper.

- If the candle burns small and bright and the wick glows, success will be forthcoming.

- If the candle burns large and bright and the wick glows, there will be exceptional good luck.

- If the candle burns dim and looks as though it would go out, there will be disillusionment, perhaps a setback in plans or relationship.

- If the candle leans to the side or the wick moves to the side, a significant change in circumstances will be experienced.

- If the candle flickers, there will definitely be a change, perhaps in finances, career or business. This may be a good omen because change brings forth creativity.

- If the candle sparkles, care should be taken with health and safety.

Candle Magick Divination

❏ If the candle twists and burns tall, it indicates there are those out to upset you, to foil your plans and place obstacles and chaos in the path of a relationship or career or financial success.

❏ If the candle dies with no outside wind source, this is a bad omen and you should heed its message. It may also mean that the answer to a question is an absolute NO.

Three Candles Set In A Triangle

Start out using the same method as above, except leave out the fourth candle in the middle of the triangle.

❏ If one candle burns more brightly than the others, the portents are good. The answer to a question is affirmative.

❏ If any of the candles have an extra bright sparkle of color at the tip of the flame, this is a very lucky omen.

❏ If the flames move from side to side, it means a change or a journey. If only one flame moves from side to side, it means a singular endeavor, an unaccompanied journey or project that must be undertaken alone.

❏ If one candle dies while the others continue to burn, there is an obstacle approaching, perhaps a sign of danger; this is definitely a warning of caution.

❏ If one of the flames spirals and twists, there may be difficulties and/or plots against you.

Candle Magick Divination

Answers To Your Questions

A very easy way to obtain an answer to a question involves the use of two small candles, such as those placed on birthday cakes. Choose their colors according to the type of question, or your personal preference.

Place these candles in their holders and stick them into a block of clay, a piece of foam or a potato, cut in half, laid cut side down. With two matches, simultaneously light the candles. Sit in front of the candles while asking your question out loud.

Because these types of candles burn out very quickly, the first to burn out reveals the answer: The left candle means: NO. The right candle means: YES.

As well, light a candle, ask a question, and observe the flame's motion. If the flame or the wick bends toward you, the answer is YES. If it bends away from you, the answer is NO.

Candle Divination On The Holidays

A technique geared to predicting the future happiness or sadness for those living in the same house can also be done using candles. This divination is traditionally performed on either Halloween, Christmas or New Year's Eve, with the purpose of revealing fortunes for the coming twelve months.

Place two candles in holders on the mantle above the fireplace or the kitchen table. Light their wicks and watch the flames' movements.

If the candles burn well with bright, long flames, good fortune for the household is predicted. If the flames are short, dim, flickers, or if they send up clouds of smoke, troubles will have to be faced. If the flame seems to burn in a normal manner, so too will life continue on its present course for those who live in the house.

To determine the character of the coming year, wait until Halloween or New Year's Eve. On that night, light a candle and go outside. Walk around your house clockwise and return inside. If you can accomplish this without the flame being extinguished the coming year will be most fortunate.

Those who have not married can see the face of their future spouse if they light one candle on Christmas day. In a darkened room, sit in front of a mirror with the candle between you and the mirror. At midnight, the face of your future love will appear in the mirror.

Candle Magick Divination

Fire And Water

Fill a small bowl half-full of water and place it on a table where you can see comfortably into it while seated. Light two purple candles and a favorite incense. Arrange the candles so their light does not reflect in the water and into your eyes. Focus your attention on the bottom of the bowl. Your hands need to be placed lightly on either side of the bowl.

Breathe gently into the water and say: "Fire and Water reveal to me that which I seek. Open my inner eye that I may truly see." Empty your mind as much as possible; remain relaxed while looking deep into the water. The answer may come in images in the water, pictures in your mind and strong bursts of "knowing."

Using the flame of the candle to show the way, write a question concerning the future on a small piece of paper. Place it face down on a flat, heat-proof surface and in front of your burning candle. Wait for five minutes and then pick the paper back up and hold it by a corner.

Light one corner of the paper with the candle flame, and then place on the fire-proof surface. If the entire paper burns, the answer is YES. If only part of the paper is destroyed, the answer is NO.

Using A Candle To Find A Lost Object

This is an ancient method somewhat akin to modern dowsing. However, instead of using forked sticks or a pendulum, you will use the flame of a candle to find what has been lost.

First, take a large candle that can be held comfortably in your hand without the risk of getting burnt by the dripping wax. The candle needs to be fresh and unused and the color should be white. Light the candle and hold it in your hand while thinking of what it is you are looking for.

With your eyes on the flame, start to turn in a circle. Look for any kind of reaction in the flame. As soon as the flame changes, stop turning and move forward. When the flame reacts again, stop and turn in a circle again. When the flame reacts, move forward. When you are near the lost object the flame will burn high and bright. Sometimes the flame may even point in the direction you need to go. Follow its lead and move carefully in that direction.

Candle Magick Divination

The Flame

Closely observe the flame on your candle. How it moves, its strength, color, and if it produces smoke can help you interpret an answer to your question. The main factor is to be observant of what the candle is trying to say to you. Open your mind and allow the candle to talk to you in its own language.

❑ **Strong Flame:** The power that you are calling forth is moving into your desires for manifestation. This strong flame shows strength in the user or the object of the spell.

❑ **Weak Flame:** On a figure candle, this could mean that the subject is losing the battle and should consider other options. This can also show that you are facing strong opposition and your magick may have to be repeated to be achieved.

❑ **Jumping Flame:** This can indicate explosions or bursts of energy being transmitted. Raw emotions or chaotic energies could be at work. An angry argument could be taking place or a heated discussion.

❑ **Rainbow Flame:** If your flame is composed of various colors this indicates that there are outside influences at work that may be beyond the power of the questioner. Colors can also show that the question may be best answered at a later date. The factors involved may need a chance to develop and evolve for a clearer view of what may occur.

Candle Magick Divination

Candles And Mirrors

Using candles and mirrors for fortune telling is an evolved form of water scrying. When it became possible to build mirrors they were regarded as being like water that was fixed into one place.

The early mirrors were made of polished copper, brass, marcasite, tin foil or mercury behind glass, polished silver and obsidian. All types of mirrors may be used for scrying and the size is not important.

Because mirrors are linked to the moon, mirrors should be backed with silver. Try and use a round or oval mirror instead of a square mirror.

For the frame try and use a mirror that has a silver frame. Old mirrors also seem to work better than new mirrors.

Most seers prefer to use a black mirror. Because this is difficult to buy you may have to make one. Simply take out the glass and paint it black. You may have to give it a few coats of paint though. When you put it back in the frame make sure the glass part is to the front.

The use of black mirrors may be traced back over the centuries. The mystic John Dee used a black mirror of obsidian to see visions and spirits. When using the black mirror for scrying you do not want to see your reflection. The best is to leave the mirror on a table and look at it from an angle.

Take two candles and place them on either side of the mirror. Make sure the room you are in is dark and quiet. Take some time to relax through meditation. Light the candles and look into the depths of the mirror as though you were looking into a bowl of water. At first it may appear grey then colors will come and go.

With time and practice you will be able to see images like still photographs or moving film images. Spirits may sometimes look at the scryer, talk to the scryer or even touch the scryer. The visions may even exist outside the mirror and surround the scryer on all sides.

A time honored Dragonstar method of scrying with a candle is to take a clear glass of water and place it in front of one lit green candle. In a darkened room, concentrate on the glass and the movements contained within as the flame burns and flickers behind the glass. Soon, you will start to see images forming in the reflections contained inside the glass. These images may show real events or meaningful symbols. Write down what you see for a later, more precise, interpretation.

Candle Magick Divination

After you have lit your candles, sit before your mirror and begin to imagine objects on its surface, one after another. You should try to see these images clearly in the mirror with your eyes open, just as if they were there in reality.

Candle Magick Divination

Crystal Ball Scrying Versus Candles And A Mirror

The term scrying comes from the English word *Descray*, which means "to perceive," "to reveal" or "to see." More than any other method, scrying with a mirror and candles instills simultaneously a sense of wonder, a sense of excitement and a sense of fear. It stirs primal memories and instinctive responses to the universe and all that affects us through it. It can be used for answering questions, self-discovery, clarification, new perspectives, accessing hidden knowledge, the past and/or the future.

The most well-known method of scrying is using a crystal ball. The crystal ball is one of the most potent avenues to higher states of consciousness. Its use in healing, activating creativity, foretelling the future and balancing the human energy system is timeless.

Through the crystal ball you can access your creative essence, reduce stress, solve problems, find lost objects, explore the mysteries of the universe and project personal energy. You can enhance your spiritual experience by adding candles, aromas and sounds. Unfortunately, a true crystal ball is hard to find and expensive. This is why the use of mirrors for scrying has become popular.

The traditional crystal ball is a wonderful tool, but a mirror along with candle magick is a more efficient way to begin to learn to scry and journey in other realms. Scrying develops one's clairvoyant abilities and is especially helpful in strengthening and opening the third eye.

As you prepare to work with your candles and mirror, always keep the surface of your mirror very clean using alcohol and a soft cloth. Never use it for anything but its intended magickal purpose. Do not let others look into its surface, Keep it stored in a safe place until needed.

Keep the working area or altar clean and free from any disturbance. Generally, scry using the mirror at night, preferably during the full or new moon, depending on the operation. The mirror can be used at any time, but some feel it tends to work better at these points. When indoors, light two votive candles, one on each side of the mirror. Use white or colored candles appropriate to the work: blue for healing, purple for psychic work, orange for communication, and so on.

Using candle magick and a scrying mirror takes practice and patience. However, the final results are well worth the extra time needed for successful divination. Don't give up if you don't see images right away, it takes time to do mirror scrying correctly.

Candle Magick Divination

Chapter Six
Shapes In The Wax

"Touch a light to the little wick, Watch it burn to the candlestick. Study with care the little blaze; Fortunes are told in its tiny rays.

If an unseen power makes it weak and low, For you it foretells a tale of woe. If that same power makes a blaze bright and healthy, You'll be happy and wise, be good and wealthy."

Ceromancy is divination from interpreting forms produced by dripping melted wax in water. Some say the best divination readings are from tarot cards or runes. However, many feel the wax and water method works best. Though it may take some practice to become successful, it is an easy process to learn.
You Will Need:

❑ **One white candle**

❑ **Matches or lighter**

❑ **A dark colored bowl filled with water**

Perform step one, Meditation. This is important as you must clear your mind of unnecessary thoughts that my cloud your interpretation of the symbols. Light your white candle and state out loud what you need to know. Hold the candle tilted over the bowl of water so the wax drips into the bowl. Watch the wax and look for symbols that might form. When you see a recognizable symbol, stop.

The drippings may even clearly spell out the answer using letters or numbers. In this case, continue until the letters or numbers stop. After you have a symbol, you must interpret it.

Candle Magick Divination

Simply take the symbol and consider what it means to you. An owl, for example, might mean sight, luck, beauty, money, etc. to you. If it spells out letters or numbers, you may not have to do any interpreting. Practice this, and you should become very effective at divining wax images.

Another popular way to do wax dripping divination was mentioned by Scott Cunningham in his book: *Earth, Air, Fire & Water*. For this you will need a number of long tapers (8 inches or longer) of the 4 basic elements, green, yellow, red and blue. One of these is necessary for every reading. You will also need a large round or square vessel filled with cold water. This can be of any material, but pottery or glass are best, for they can withstand heat. Plastic is not recommended.

Put the candles, a book or matches or lighter and the vessel of water on a table or other flat surface. If you have a particular question you want answered, use the appropriate candle color. If you are not sure of the proper color, use white. If you have no question but are simply desiring a glimpse into your future, use yellow, for this is the color of divination in general.

Light the candle and hold it upright over the water for a moment, thinking about your question or simply calming your mind. When the candle is fully flaming and has begun melting the wax, tilt it and hold steadily about an inch over the water's surface. The wax will begin dripping onto the water.

If the tiny drips (which harden into small droplets of wax, smooth on the top but round on the bottom) do not merge and create a pattern, you aren't concentrating on the question. Sweep all else from your mind.

The wax drops will form a pattern on the surface of the water. If you are having trouble achieving this, begin moving the candle slowly, allowing the drops to touch one another and so to form a line on the water. If this is done for a few minutes a definite shape will appear on the water. When this happens quench the candles flame with your fingers or a candle-snuffer and set aside.

Look at the shape. What does it look like? Pick it up carefully so as not to break it and turn it over. Does it look the same or different? Study its thickness to see if it says anything to you symbolically.

Some common forms that the wax can take are: **Spirals** - These are the most common, because of the way the wax rotates on the surface of the water, spirals represent reincarnation, the universe, the world or perhaps a particular life. It could mean you need to evolve beyond it, or that it is something from a previous life.

Candle Magick Divination

Perhaps, depending on the nature of the question, the problem or its solution is in the home. This is an excellent example of how interpretation must be a personal thing, no one else can tell you exactly how these symbols relate to you. Usually the first meaning that comes into your mind is the correct one.

Circles: Circles represent eternity and fertility, and both of these attributes can be interpreted according to the question asked. Fertility would perhaps represent a new activity, financial security, or even a new baby on the way. It may also signify the successful completion of a project.

Eternity may mean just that - it will be a long time before something is completed or comes to pass. Circles also represent religion and spirituality, and thus can be seen in this context during interpretation.

Broken Lines: If the wax drops form into lines but they aren't connected, it represents a scattering of forces, or lack of focus in your life, business or other pursuits. It can also signify forces working against you. but don't take this too literally – such 'forces' may well be within your own being. This isn't a positive pattern to find, for it is a sign that changes must be made to bring order into your life.

Dots: Dots, unconnected wax drops, sometimes are the only thing you can get. As stated above, this sometimes signifies lack of attention to the divination, but it can also mean that the problem is too complex for an answer at this time. If you try wax divination several times with only dots coming up each time, you're either asking the wrong questions, or if you haven't asked one, you shouldn't be seeking a glimpse into your future at this time, at least not through wax and water.

Wax Divination For A Group

To perform divination with candles for a group, you will need a small bowl filled with cool water, a variety of colored candles, matches or a lighter, and an open mind. Put a white candle by each side of the bowl. Set the bowl on an alter or table where it can easily be reached by each person present.

Have each person present select a colored candle. Have the participants choose the questions they want answered by the divination beforehand, so the question can be matched with the appropriate candle color. Red is used for love and relationships; green for prosperity, career, or jobs; yellow for school, study, creativity, and mental pursuits;

Candle Magick Divination

light blue for health and recovery from illness; violet for spiritual growth; pink for friendships, children, and pets; orange for changes and possible moves; and white for general life pattern. Before the participants light their candles for divination, have each of them call upon an ancestor whom they liked for aid.

To begin, have one person at a time light a candle of his or her choice. Gently stir the water in the bowl in a clockwise direction, then have the person with the candle let the wax slowly drip into the water while thinking of the question to be answered.

Patterns in the wax are scanned for symbols that will answer the question. If any of the wax symbols break apart or are indistinct, the meaning is modified. After each reading, take out the used wax so as not to confuse the next reading.

If you see tiny drops individually placed on top of the water's surface, more concentration is needed. You may need to slowly move the candle around for a short time. After a shape or symbol of sorts has formed, quench the candle's flame with a snuffer or your finger tips. Never blow or shake it out.

If you see a circle shape, there can be many possibilities. A circle may represent spirituality, the cycle of life, or even fertility. Interpreted, it may mean that something exciting and new is on its way, or a task at hand will take some time to complete. It all depends on what it means to you.

Spirals or swirls represent rebirth. Perhaps your question is about a past life, and how you wish to interpret its meanings. Dots continue to symbolize your lack of concentration on the spell. Try your best to clear your mind of all ideas not associated with the reading. Small lines usually tend to represent disorder, and some negativity.

Traditional Wax Symbols

Like reading tea leaves or coffee grounds, the shapes produced by dripping wax into water are open for your own private symbolism. As you become more proficient with interpreting the types of shapes produced by the wax, you will soon recognize familiar shapes and their personal meaning to you. Don't be disappointed if at first all you seem to get are dots, blobs and lines. It takes practice to produce the more complicated shapes associated with wax divination. Until you create your own personal meanings to the shapes, here is a list of traditional shapes produced by wax drippings and their accepted meanings.

Candle Magick Divination

Airplane or Boat - A trip of disappointment.

Anchor - Your loved one is true.

Baby - Troubles are coming soon.

Ball or Balloon - Your problem will not last very long.

Beans - Money difficulties.

Bed - A vacation would be good for you.

Bells - A wedding is in your future.

Bird - News will reach you soon.

Bridge - Take a chance, you'll never know unless you try.

Broom - Make a change, it will be for the better.

Butterfly - Fickle friends, an unreliable person.

Candle - Spiritual growth is required if you want something to happen.

Cat - A friend is untrue, or could be spreading lies about you.

Chain - Go ahead with your plans, you are on the right course.

Circle - Reconciliation and forgiveness.

Candle Magick Divination

Cloud - Something or someone threatens you.

Cross - Do not fear for you are protected.

Crown - Sickness either for yourself or someone close to you.

Cup - Bitter quarrel with a friend. You could be wrong, so check your facts.

Dagger - Danger, treachery, recklessness.

Dish - Unbroken: contentment and plenty.

Dish - Broken: problems at home.

Dog - Your self-esteem is too low, lighten up on yourself and enjoy life. Take some time out strictly for yourself.

Ear - Be alert for an opportunity to advance in your work.

Egg - New developments soon. A good time to start fresh. A baby could be on the way.

Fan - A surprise is in store for you.

Feather - The problem will soon be solved.

Fish - Someone will betray you.

Forked line - An important decision is to be made.

Candle Magick Divination

Gate: Future success.

Ghost - Someone from the past is looking for you.

Grass - Good fortune is approaching after a long period of bad luck.

Hat - A change of location is indicated.

Hand - Open: new friendships.

Hand - Closed: opportunity lost, arguments.

Heart - A friendship will turn into love.

House - Better times are coming so hang on and don't despair. This may show a change in your life for the better.

Key - A setback in plans should be expected.

Kite - Your wish will not come true. Maybe this is not what you really want, so examine your true needs and desires.

Ladder - Take steps to change your attitude toward an old friend.

Leaf or Leaves - Things will be changing soon for the better. Your wishes will finally come true.

Lines - Straight: no barriers in getting ahead.

Candle Magick Divination

Lines - Broken: obstacles.

Lines - Wavy: uncertain path.

Lion - An unpleasant situation is developing. It is up to you to get yourself out of trouble as soon as possible.

Moon - Indicates more money is coming your way.

Mountains - Good friends and family members are willing to help you with your problem.

Pants - You will be tempted. Don't give in to temptation or wishful thinking. It will not make you happy.

Pen - Expect a letter from a relative.

Pin - Your lover may be attracted to another.

Pipe - Peace and comfort.

Question mark - Need for caution.

Ring - Marriage may be possible in the near future.

Ring - Broken: divorce, separation.

Scales - Legal matters.

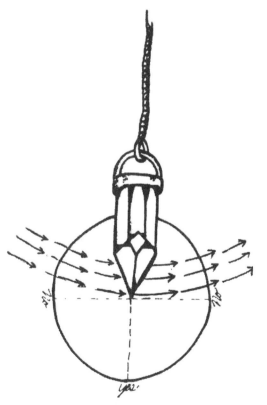

Candle Magick Divination

Scissors - Separation, a difficult break-up, divorce.

Shoe - Be suspicious of a new acquaintance. They could be hiding something from you.

Snake - Be on guard against an enemy who is plotting against you. This person could be someone close to you.

Spider Web - Pleasant happenings and good fortune.

Star - Happiness and contentment.

Sun - Good fortune after a period of bad.

Table - An abundance of blessings.

Tent - A move to a new home.

Tree - A good time for new undertakings.

Umbrella - Trouble is coming.

Walking Stick - Get out of the house and visit friends.

Wheel - One who has been away will return soon with important news.

Wings - Messages.

Witch - Danger will pass you by.

Candle Magick Divination

A German Holiday Tradition Using Lead And Wax

On Sankt Sylvester day (News Years Day), celebrated on December 31. Germans sing songs of thanksgiving. Punch is served with jelly doughnuts. For fun, some doughnuts are filled with mustard.

Later that evening, family members and friends have a ceremony, which consists of holding a lump of lead in a spoon over a lamp, or fire place. When the lead melts, they dump it into cold water. An adult is selected to be the fortune teller who predicts the future from the shape of the cooler lead. Today, many families use wax instead.

A Special Dragonstar Method To Divine With Wax

Another method to divine the future for yourself, or others, was developed long ago by the then living Dragonstar. In a quiet room, take one red candle and hold it with both of your hands. Say out loud to the candle what it is you are wanting to learn. If you desire to see images of your future, ask to see your future.

Keep your questions simple and to the point. Now light the candle and allow it to burn seven minutes while you concentrate on the flame. Take the candle and very carefully allow the wax to drip onto a piece of paper.

Quickly take the paper, fold it in two and allow the wax to dry. Unfold the paper and look inside at the wax. Check for symbolic shapes that should provide answers to your questions. If the shapes are uncertain, the time is not right to answer your questions, and you should ask again later.

Another interesting method involves answering a YES or NO question with melted candle wax. Simply draw two large circles on a piece of paper, one for YES and the other NO. Write your question along the bottom of the paper. Turn the paper upside down so you cannot see the marked side.

Take one blue candle and light it. Hold the candle in front of you and ask your question into the flame. Watch the fire for any changes, such as a flicker, or growing brighter or dimmer.

When you feel the candle is ready, tip it so that a few drops of wax fall onto the paper below. Place the candle back into its holder and pick up the paper and hold it in front of the candle. The wax on the paper will silhouette through the paper. The circle that has the largest concentration of wax drops will answer your question.

Candle Magick Divination

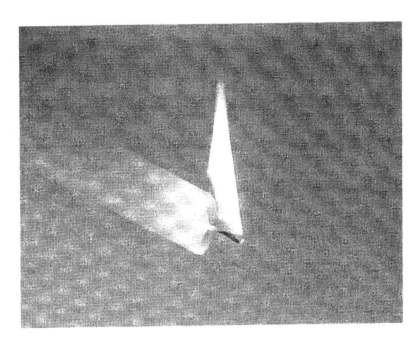

Many feel the wax and water technique of divination works better than other traditional methods such as the Tarot.

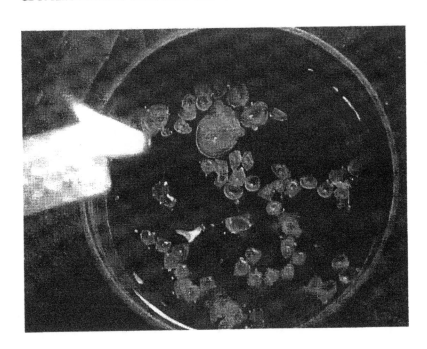

Chapter Seven
Fire - Smoke & Ashes

Ancient man spent many hours sitting around the campfire watching the magical flames dance around the fire pit long into the night. It's hardly surprising then that divining with fire, **Pyromancy**, became one of the first methods developed by early man to look into the mysteries of the future.

Gazing through half-closed eyes into the glowing embers, they were frequently able to make contact with the mysteries of the universe and gain insight into that which could not be known. Fire oscillates between the actual and the possible, between dreams and reality. These ancient perceptions can still be brought into use today with the same clarity that assisted our ancestors into mystical visions of other realities.

Any number of people can read their own fortunes in the same fire, for the formations of the embers appear differently to each person, and are also interpreted by that person in their own individual way. This is the sort of divination that is best suited to do for yourself.

If you are doing fire divination for someone else, then sit with that person on your left; their right hand held between your own two hands as you gaze into the fire. Spend a few moments attuning to that person before focusing your gaze into the fire itself.

It may be that, no matter how long you gaze into the fire, you can see nothing that seems to have any real meaning to you. This is not necessarily an unfavorable sign but simply means that the forces at work are presently changing rapidly and have not settled into any sort of a complete picture. Give up and try again later. Don't fire-gaze for longer than ten minutes at one time.

Time is judged by position: any symbol near the top of the fire is in the present; the lower down the fire it appears, the further into the future it will be. Those symbols on the left of the fire are more likely to be negative symbols, while those on the right are more likely to be positive.

Also the way a symbol faces may well have a specific meaning. Symbols facing you will have a direct effect; facing away, an indirect effect. Don't expect all the symbols to look exactly like the things they represent. You will have to use your imagination a great deal. You will find that there is usually just a suggestion of, say, a bird or a rabbit. Use the symbols simply as a focal point and go with your psychic feelings.

Candle Magick Divination

The Ways of Pyromancy

There are many interesting ways to use fire to divine the future. In his book *Earth Power*, author Scott Cunningham writes that one easy way to divine from flames is to set a fire and watch how quickly the wood begins to burn. If it catches the flame quickly, it is a good sign, and you should proceed with the divination. If the fire is hesitant, or if you need to use several matches to get even the smallest twig to light, abandon the project until another time.

Some say that if the fire lights quickly it is a sign that visitors are on their way. Others say that if the fire is difficult to light, rain is to be expected. Once the fire is actually blazing, watch its flames carefully.

❑ If the fire burns to one side of the fireplace, or pit, or area, love may be in the air.

❑ Much crackling indicates misfortune ahead; perform protective spells.

❑ A distinct hollow in the midst of the flames foretells an ending of a problem bothering you.

❑ If the fire suddenly roars up the chimney or up into the air for no apparent reason, an argument may soon occur. Watch your words carefully.

❑ Sparks on the back of the chimney or, if outside, flying aggressively up into the air mean that important news is on the way.

❑ If a loved one is far from home, poke at the fire with a poker or stick. If shafts of flame shoot up, you can be assured that he or she is well, safe, and happy.

❑ If three bolts of flame rise up and burn separately, expect a momentous event to occur soon in your life.

Candle Magick Divination

Fire Scrying Chant

Sit before a fire and relax. Close your eyes and still your consciousness. Reopen your eyes and look straight into the fire. Do not stare. Breathe deeply and when at peace say these or similar words in a low voice:

"Blazing fire As you dance Give me now the Secret glance Call upon my Second Sight Make me psychic.

"With your light Blazing fire Shining bright Give me now the Second Sight" Repeat this until your eyes grow heavy. Divine the future in the restless flames."

Once the fire has died to a glowing reddish-white mass of coals, stare into its heart. If you wish, throw some Fire of **Azrael** incense onto the coals (equal parts cedar, juniper and sandalwood). This will flare up & burn, but will quickly die down.

With the scented smoke rising from the divination incense look deep into the fiery coals. See what shapes the charred wood seem to form, and determine their meaning through the language of symbolism.

A Favorite Fire Spell From Lady Sha`leen

Lady Sha`leen has written that this spell is particularly well cast while sitting before the Yule Log, but is just as effective with any fire. While watching the flames, repeat this verse three times:

Fire red and burning well,
Into your depths I cast this spell,
Knowing that indeed full well,
My future here thee will me tell.

Then, poke the fire three times.

Candle Magick Divination

Sit before a roaring fire and ask a question. Gaze into the flames while the fire burns down. Within the flames, or in the sparkling, glowing coals below them, images and symbols of the future may appear before you.

Candle Magick Divination

Watch the way in which the sparks fly up just after you have spoken the incantation. Generally, fast plentiful sparks and spits mean a hectic start to the new spring, with a lot to do and little time to do it. Several loud pops mean shocks to a current way of life, perhaps the appearance of a mentor. Slow, burning hisses indicates that you should take time out by yourself for contemplation and self reflection.

Fire Gazing

This ancient technique can produce surprising results. Sit before a roaring fire. Ask your question. Gaze into the flames while the fire burns down. Within the flames, or in the sparkling, glowing coals below them, images of the future may appear. Interpret them with symbolic thought. It's best to limit gazing time to about five minutes, but there's no need to check your watch. Allow the images to come to you for an appropriate time.

An alternate version of fire gazing consists of lighting a fire and reading the future according to its appearance. If, after stirring the fire, it burns brightly, a loved one far from home is safe and happy. Pale flames foretell the approach of bad weather. If the fire suddenly blazes up hot and bright, a stranger will soon arrive. Blue flames indicate the approach of a bad storm.

Showers of sparks from a fire indicate that news of some importance will reach you shortly. When the fire seems to be buzzing (as opposed to crackling), storms are at hand. Sparks flying from the fire indicate a coming fight in the household. If a fire refuses to light, hard work will be needed in the future. If the fire lights quickly, visitors are to be expected. A very bright fire is a sure sign of rain. A sputtering fire means snow is on its way. When the fire talks, trouble is ahead.

Purification With Flames

If you wish to be free from a habit, thought, or set of ideas; if you wish to be rid of past associations, guilt or blockages; take the symbols of that problem, whether they be overeating, smoking, drinking, and throw them onto a raging fire. As the fire consumes the symbols, so shall it consume the power they had over you. For more abstract problems, draw a symbol or image on a piece of paper and burn it.

Candle Magick Divination

To Help Cure What Ails You

Light a fire, oak wood, if possible. When much of the wood has been reduced to glowing embers, pick up one carefully with a pair of tongs or shovel and throw it immediately into a cauldron or pot of cold water. It will sizzle and pop. As it does, visualize the disease leaving the body of the afflicted person. Repeat this operation three more times.

Anti-Fire Charm

To protect your home from a destructive fire, place some mistletoe in a blue drawstring bag, douse it thoroughly with cold, clear water, and then immediately hang it in the "heart" of the house – where you and your family spend most of your time. Or, light a piece of wood and burn to ash. Wet the ashes, let them dry, and hang in a blue drawstring bag.

Spell Of Protection

Sit or stand before any fire. Look into the flames. Visualize the fire bathing you with glowing, protective light. The fire creates a flaming, shimmering sphere around you that weaves a web of all powerful protection. If you wish, say the following or similar words:

Craft the spell in the fire;
Craft it well; Weave it higher.
Weave it now of shining flame;
None shall come to hurt or maim.
None shall pass this fiery wall;
None shall pass No, none at all.

Repeat this simple yet effective ritual every day when in need.

Candle Magick Divination

A Spell For Fiery Love

Create or find a charred stick. You will also need a few dried rose petals and a piece of paper. Using the charred part of the stick as you would a pencil, draw two inter-linked hearts on paper as you visualize yourself enjoying a satisfying relationship. Draw with power.

Hold the rose petals in your projecting hand and send fiery, loving energies into them. Sprinkle the petals over the linked hearts. Do this with power. Wrap the package around the petals. Still visualizing, throw the package into a fire. As it burns, the power is released into the universe.

Healing Fire With A Red Candle

Draw a picture of yourself with the disease, wound or condition. Clearly point out the problem in the picture.

Charge a red candle with healing energy. Light the candle's wick. Hold the tip of the picture in the flame. After it is lit, drop it into a fire proof container. Now, with the red candle still burning, draw another picture of yourself without the ailment. Place this picture under the red candle and let it burn out.

Daphnomancy

Daphnomancy is another form of fire divination that consists of tossing laurel branches or leaves into a fire. To find the answer to a yes or no question, say the following directly to the fire.

Fire, fire, blessed fire,
Unto fortune I aspire.
Now I hope that I may see,
The future that will come to me.

Then state your question while tossing five bay leaves on the fire. If they crackle and splutter while burning, the answer is YES. If they burn silently, the answer is NO.

Candle Magick Divination

You can also throw a flammable object, other than laurel leaves, into the fire while asking a question. If it doesn't burn or if it burns more slowly than usual, the signs are favorable, or the answer is yes. If it does burn, unfavorable or no.

Wooden matches also play a role in fire divination. Ask a yes or no question. Light a match and hold it straight up. If the head curves toward the left while burning, the answer is no. If to the right, yes.

Smoke Readings

Where there is fire, there's smoke. Because of their inseparable nature, smoke has also played the role of fortune teller for those seeking answers to the future. Libanomancy is the observation of smoke as it rises from a fire, from burning objects or from incense. The Babylonians and Greeks who performed it carefully watched the smoke rising from the burning food offered in sacrifice to their deities.

Simply light one candle and pass a plain white card through the flames three times while asking a question. You must do this quickly to avoid setting the card on fire. Interpret the resulting carbon deposits left on the underside of the card using your personal symbolic keys.

There are some older techniques that stretch back beyond written language. For example, build a fire outside in a safe place while asking a yes/no question. Watch the smoke. If it rises straight and lightly into the air, a positive answer has been received. If, however, it hangs heavily around the fire, the reverse is true.

Another way involves the burning of specific objects and observing the smoke that rises from them. Asking your question, throw a handful of poppy seeds onto the burning coals of a dying fire. If the smoke rises straight and lightly into the air, it means YES. If the smoke hangs close to the fire the answer is NO.

You can also throw a handful of cedar shavings onto the coals while asking your question and, once again, read the omens according to the method described above.

An easier technique requires nothing more exotic than burning an incense stick. Though any type can be used, sandalwood seems to produce the best results, plus it smells great. Hold the incense stick between your hands and ask your question. Light it, set it in its holder, and gaze into the smoke. A message may be revealed to you by the smoke's appearance or actions.

Candle Magick Divination

Bark Divination

Take a broad, thin piece of bark and place it into a bright fire until it catches flame. When it starts to burn, quickly set it a little distance from the fire.

When it has stopped burning, carefully stare at the symbols visible in the charred ash-laden wood.

Ashes

Before the opulence of modern life turned us into the "throw-away everything" society, people made use of just about anything and everything that was made available. This includes fire divination using ashes after the fire has finally died out. The final product of fire's transforming properties, ashes were once highly respected and can still be used to determine the future.

Collect ashes from dead fires or the fire place. Outside, in a place where the wind usually blows at some time, scatter the ashes to a good depth in a rectangular shape on the ground.

While asking your question regarding the future, use a finger to write the word yes in the ashes to the right and no to the left. Leave them undisturbed overnight. In the morning, study the ashes. If both words are clearly legible, no answer is possible at this time. If one has been erased by animal tracks, the wind or by some other force, the remaining word reveals the answer to your question. If both words are gone, again, no answer has been given.

You can also write in the ashes two or three words that represents your question, such as "Will I Find Love Soon?" The next morning you'll probably find that some of the letters have been destroyed. Piece together the remaining letters to reveal the future.

The following is a special technique developed over the years by the Dragonstar Continuum to divine the future using Tarot cards and smoke from incense. This method requires that you read your cards in a quiet room free from breezes.

First, light your favorite incense. We have found that cone or stick incense produces the best smoke. Next, shuffle your cards while concentrating on your question. Observe the smoke rising from the incense. When the smoke begins to ripple or move about, stop shuffling and lay your cards out. Pay attention to the smoke while reading the cards. Changes in the smoke at certain cards signifies closer attention to that card.

Candle Magick Divination

An easy technique for smoke divination involves the burning of an incense stick. Hold the incense stick between your hands and ask a question. If the smoke rises straight into the air, the answer is YES. If it curls and swirls in the air, the answer is NO.

Chapter Eight
Flames And Folklore

Fire is very important to mankind. It has consistently played a major role in human production and life. It could be said that the discovery of the use of fire was genuinely an event of epoch-making progress.

Over the centuries, superstitions and omens have developed around the use of fire and the vessels used to contain fire for personal benefit. To our ancestors, candles and lamps were often the only source of light, and the best way to interpret omens.

If the candle-flame burns blue and dim, it is considered a sign that a spirit is passing, although in some places a blue flame indicates frost on the way. A bright spark in the wick means a letter for the person nearest the candle, or sometimes the arrival of a visitor.

Weather was also foretold by candle-flame; a flame which flickers and wavers when there is no breeze means windy weather is on the way, whereas a candle which will not light easily indicates rain.

It was thought unlucky to light a candle from the hearth. Candles should also be blown out before they burned out, for if they were allowed to gutter out in the candlestick it was said that a sailor would die at sea.

To snuff a candle out accidentally was an omen of a wedding. Three candles should never be lit from a single match or taper, and to have three candles burning in one room was very ill-omened, although in some parts of Britain it foretold a wedding. In other places people who sat together in a room with three candles lit would quarrel.

It was considered unlucky to leave a candle to burn in an empty room. However, a large candle was often left burning through the night of Christmas Eve in order to ensure prosperity, warmth and light throughout the coming year; this custom has its origins in the pre-Christian festival of Yule.

Reading omens from fire was practiced by the ancient Chinese with the Torch Festival of the Yi, Bai, Naxi, Lili and Hani nations. This was recorded in the records of Yunnan Tongzhi (The Annals of Yunnan).

The records state that by "making pine torches on June 25 and carrying the torches to the crop field, people predict the result of the harvest by the color of the torch fire." The Yi people of Liangshan used to put mustard seeds into fire to predict the harvest.

Candle Magick Divination

A good harvest was told when the seeds cracked in fire. The Pumi people believed that a vigorous flame with sparkle in the fireplace was a propitious sign, indicating the arrival of a rare visitor or good fortune.

On the other hand, it indicated bad luck if the flame kept flickering. Fire was also used to chase away devils and to resist disasters when pestilence spread. The Jingpo nationality, when conducting fire divination, put into fire a piece of bamboo with joints at both ends. It would indicate propitiousness if the bamboo cracked with only one end bending upwards, while it would be considered a bad omen when both ends bent upwards.

The Hearth

Before the introduction of modern forms of heating, the hearth was the symbolic and often literal center of the house. In ancient times the fire burnt in the middle of the main room, where it served for cooking and heating and symbolically stood for the source of life.

In ancient times the fire was never allowed to go out; the phrase "a desolate hearth" also meant an abandoned house, a scattered family, lost kinfolk. A bride would be led to the hearth of her new home and the fire-irons put into her hand to symbolize her new status as mistress of the house.

Among the Bulang people of ancient China, weddings, and ceremonies for adulthood and adoption were all held around the fireplace. Among the Yi people of Xiaoliangshan (Small Cool Mountain), a ceremony called: *Being Dressed in Trousers* would be held around the fireplace for boys who reached a certain age.

A stone would first be heated in the fireplace and then sprinkled with cold water after it was taken out. The trousers then were rotated in the steam produced from the stone and were put on by the boy with the mother's help, while prayers were chanted by the group.

Throughout the year the live cinders in the fireplace should not be allowed to be extinguished. When moving house, they must be carried to the new abode. If by any chance the cinders went out or were contaminated, a new kindling had to be obtained through the use of the primitive wood-boring method. The wood used for this purpose must be especially selected in order to preserve the fire's holiness and purity.

Candle Magick Divination

Among the Jinuo, Wa and Tai nationalities, the first thing to do upon the settlement of a new household is to set up a new fireplace with the performance of special ceremonies. The Tai people had many restrictions having to do with the construction of a new fireplace. The fireplace should have four sides of equal length, four corners of equal angle, with flowers put at each corner and egg shells put on top of the flowers.

Once the fireplace was constructed, the male head of the household erected the tripod pot-holder while the female head made the fire. Relatives and friends would gather for a congratulation in which the old man expert at the ceremony would sing the Fireplace Song, which included the lines: "The foundation is like gold plate; the fireplace silver pit; the fence of the house will ever remain untouched by borers; and the central pillar of the house will last for ever." It can be seen from this that the Tai people regarded the fireplace as the source of their good fortune.

In addition, taboos regarding fireplace homage have been maintained by the ethnic groups in the region. The most common taboos are that it is not permissible to cross over the fireplace, or to move the tripod pot-holder at random, or to walk on it.

In Scotland and Ireland the open peat fires were often ritually raked at night; this was a complicated ceremony involving the division of the embers into three separate parts with a small heap in the middle, each of which had a peat laid in it, the whole thing then being covered with just enough ashes to keep the fire quiet without extinguishing it. Generally performed by the woman of the house, this ritual was intended for protection of the entire household and sleeping family, symbolized by the subdued fire.

It is still often considered unlucky to poke someone else's fire without permission, unless one had known the householder well for at least seven years. Until the last century it was also considered in some parts of Britain to be unlucky to give fire, or even a light, out of one's house on New Year's Day; if fire was given it was said that a death would follow within the year.

The behavior of a fire in the grate is the source of many omens. If the fire burns all on one side, or falls into two heaps in the grate, a parting is foretold; if it will not start in the morning it foretells quarrels in the house, and quarrels are also foretold from a spluttering piece of coal.

A coffin-shaped piece of coal flying out of the fire and into the room foretells a death, whereas a cradle-shaped piece means a birth. If the flames are bluish, or very high, it means that frosty weather is coming. A cluster of bright sparks at the back of the chimney means good news on the way, and dull sparks means bad news.

Candle Magick Divination

The behavior of a fire in the grate is the source of many omens. If the fire burns all on one side, a parting is foretold; if it will not start in the morning it foretells quarrels in the house, and quarrels are also foretold from a spluttering piece of coal.

Candle Magick Divination

The Magick And Folklore Of Fire & Herbs

Herbs have long been thought to have a touch of magick. Certain superstitions and folklore surrounding herbs detail their mystical interaction with fire in the form of omens and divination.

BASIL (Ocimum Basilicum)

The scent of fresh basil causes sympathy between two people and therefor can be used to soothe tempers. This herb is added to love incenses and sachets. The fresh herb is rubbed against the skin as a form of natural love perfume. Basil is also used in love divinations, but care must be taken that the person of your affections is not unnaturally swayed by your magick. Place two fresh basil leaves on a live coal. If they lie where you put them and burn quickly to ashes the relationship will be harmonious. If there is a certain amount of crackling, the life of the pair will be disturbed by quarrels. If the leaves fly apart the pairing is undesirable.

LAVENDAR (Lavendula officinale or L.vera)

Lavender has been used in love spells and clothing rubbed with the flower attracts love. A piece of paper on which lavender has been rubbed is excellent for attraction. The flowers are also burned or smolder to induce sleep and rest. It can be scattered around the home to maintain peacefulness. The odor of Lavender is conductive for a long life. The herb is also used in healing mixtures and carried to see ghosts or worn to protect against the evil eye.

Patchouli (Pogostemon cablin or P.patchouli)

This herb smells like rich earth and so can be used in money and prosperity mixtures. It can be sprinkled onto money added to purses and wallets and placed around the base of green candles being used for candle magick.

THYME (Thymus vulgaris)

This herb is burned to attract good health and can also be worn for this purpose. Placed beneath the pillow, it ensures restful sleep and pleasant dreams with no nightmares or obsessive thoughts to keep you awake. Thyme also can aid in developing psychic powers.

Candle Magick Divination

The Midsummer's Fire

In pagan Europe villages would ignite a great bonfire into which they sometimes threw effigies of witches, or burned animals like cattle or witch-identified creatures like cats. In fact, the name "Bonfire" derives from the term "bonefire."

Through the bonfire's smoke, and over its ebbing flames or coals, the villagers passed their flocks, cattle stricken by murrain, most commonly, but also pigs, geese, and horses in set order.

Then, they themselves would go through the dying bonfire. Next they carried the flame and smoke with torches through the countryside; their fields, orchards, and pastures. The ashes were sometimes scattered over the ground, and sometimes pressed over their faces. They carried the embers or tapers to their homes to re-ignite the hearth, and kept the extinguished brand in the house as a talisman against lightning, wildfire, and witchcraft.

The Midsummer's fire persisted far past the ancient days of paganism as was recorded in nineteenth-century Ireland in the book: *Ancient Legends, Mystic Charms; and Superstitions of Ireland* by Lady Wilde.

"The sacred fire was lighted with great ceremony on Midsummer Eve; and on that night all the people of the adjacent country kept fixed watch on the western promontory of Howth, and the moment the first flash was seen from that spot the fact of ignition was announced with wild cries and cheers repeated from village to village, when all the local fires began to blaze, and Ireland was circled by a cordon of flame rising up from every hill.

"Then the dance and song began round every fire, and the wild hurrahs filled the air with the most frantic revelry. Many of these ancient customs are still continued, and the fires are still lighted on St. John's Eve on every hill in Ireland.

"When the fire has burned down to a red glow the young men striped to the waist and leap over or through the flames; this is done backwards and forwards several times, and he who braves the greatest blaze is considered the victor over the powers of evil, and is greeted with tremendous applause.

"When the fire burns still lower the young girls leap the flame, and those who leap clean over three times back and forward will be certain of a speedy marriage and good luck with many children. The married women then walk through the lines of the burning embers; and when the fire is nearly burnt and trampled down, the yearling cattle are driven through the hot ashes, and their back is singed with a lighten hazel twig. These rods are kept safely afterwards, being considered of immense power to drive the cattle to and from the watering places.

"As the fire diminishes the shouting grows fainter, and the song and dance commence; while professional story-tellers narrate tales of fairy-land, or of the good old times long ago, when the kings and princes of Ireland dwelt amongst their own people, and there was food to eat and wine to drink for all comers to the feast at the king's house.

"When the crowd at length separate, every one carries home a brand from the fire, and great virtue is attached to the lighted brone which is safely carried to the house without breaking or falling to the ground. Many contests also arise amongst the young men; for whoever enters his house first with the sacred fire brings the good luck of the year with him."

Keep The Christmas Fires Burning

The Yule log may have originated with the Druids and early Scandinavians. To ancient tribes, fire was a symbol of the home and safety. In the cold and gloomy days of deepest winter, huge fires would be lit to burn out the sins of the past year.

The Scandinavians believed the sun was attached to a big wheel (HWEOL) that stops for twelve days during the winter solstice, so they lit the fire to last for the entire period. The Celts also believed that the sun stood still for twelve days during the winter solstice. In order for the power of light to conquer the darkness, the Druids would bless a log, the Yule log, and keep it burning for twelve days.

The English took on the custom, by burning a yule log on Christmas Eve. Partying, singing, and group activities surrounded the entire ritual from beginning to end, creating the "Yuletide" atmosphere that remains today, even in homes without a fireplace or yule log to burn.

The log must be obtained by the family itself, not bought from someone else. It had to be lighted with a piece of last year's Yule log. It must burn continuously for the twelve days of Christmas. If your shadow cast by the light of the Yule log fire seemed to be headless, you would die within one year. The log's ashes could cure ailments and was believed to avert lightning.

Candle Magick Divination

It was considered good luck to sit on the Yule log before it was burned. It was bad luck if the fire went out quickly. After the holidays had ended, a piece of the log was saved to rekindle next year's log.

If the log went out during the twelve days of Christmas, great misfortune might be brought about. Keeping a small piece to light the yule log next winter would ensure that good luck and prosperity was carried on from year to year.

The berry of the Bay Tree, which is often used in the fragrant candles lit every Christmas. Legend has it that the Bay Tree gave shelter to the holy family during a storm. Therefore, lightning is said to never strike it. Sweethearts who light bayberry candles when they are separated at Christmas time will supposedly be united by way of the gentle scent.

The Christmas observances in East Yorkshire are always looked upon as a time of joy even by the poorest. On Christmas Eve the houses are decked with "hollin" or other evergreens, which are never burnt afterwards, but thrown away.

The Yule log used to be brought in and placed upon the fire along with a piece of log left over from the previous year. The old log had been carefully preserved for good luck, in much the same way as the Yuletide candle.

The Christmas candle is always a feature in the furnishing of the feast. It is lighted by the head of the house, and generally stands in the center of the table, round which the members of the family sit to partake of the food and other dainties that deck the board.

No other candle must be lighted from it, and before the family retire to rest the master of the house blows it out, leaving what remains of it to stand where it is until the following morning. The unconsumed piece is then carefully stowed away with other similar relics of former years; sometimes quite a large number of such pieces are accumulated in the course of years: it is considered in some localities highly unlucky to disturb these remnants during the year.

It was further thought unlucky not only, as I have said, to take a light from the Yule candle, but also to give a light to any one on Christmas Day; so that in former times, before matches were invented as we have them now, the question used to be asked before retiring to rest on Christmas Eve, "Is your tunder dhry?"

In former times the Yule candle was looked upon as almost a sacred thing. If by any chance it went out, it was believed that some member of the family would die during the ensuing year.

Candle Magick Divination

Omens Of The Flame

Dreaming of fire is considered to be an omen of good fortune, happiness and hope for the future.

Whenever a bird flew into a window at night when a candle was burning, it signified that someone very close would soon be dead. If ashes from a stove or fireplace were carried out on New Year's Day it meant that a dead person would be carried out during the year.

If a cat sits with its back to the fire, expect a frost. If the cat instead sits facing the fire, expect warmer weather to arrive.

If burning coals stick to the bottom of a pot, it is the sign of a tempest. Fires burning paler than usual and murmuring within are significant of storms. Burning wood pops more before rain and snow. If smoke falls to the ground, it is likely to rain. Campfires are more smoky before a rain.

If a person's hair burns brightly when thrown in the fire, it is a sign of long life - the brighter the flame, the longer the life.

Never put out with your finger the little red spark that tries to linger on the wick of a blown-out candle: just so long as it burns, some soul in purgatory enjoys rest from torment. The spark in the wick is called a " letter" and foretells the arrival of good news.

If the candle-flame burns blue and dim, it is considered a sign that a spirit is passing, although in some places a blue flame indicates frost on the way. A bright spark in the wick means a letter for the person nearest the candle, or sometimes the arrival of a visitor.

A knot in the wick, burning with a red glow, indicates the visit of a stranger. A wick charred but remaining over the flame is a sign of good luck. To kill a lone moth hovering about a candle is a harbinger of good luck. Never light three candles with one

Candle Magick Divination

match...nor have just three candles burning, although in some parts of Britain it foretold a wedding. In other places people who sat together in a room with three candles lit would quarrel.

When the wax of a candle takes the shape of a handle, this is called a "Coffin handle," and portends bad luck. A lover could be called to visit by thrusting two pins into a lit candle and reciting a charm over it.

According to Jewish legend, there is a connection between fire, which is a sacred symbol of life and fertility, and the child while it is still in its mother's womb. In talmudic times such importance was attached to the lighting of candles for a woman in childbed that the rabbis permitted it even on the Sabbath, and even for a blind woman if she asked that a birth candle be lit during her delivery. That detail shows that the candle served as a charm for ensuring successful delivery and as a protection for the lives of mother and child.

The same purpose was served by lighting a fire for the woman in childbed for thirty days, "even in the period of Tammuz" (that is, in midsummer when it was certainly not needed for warmth). In ancient Rome they lighted a candle in the room of the woman in confinement to drive away the demons, and the same custom is practiced in modern Greece.

Native Hawaiians believe that to dream of fire consuming a house meant there would be a false charge against the dreamer. If the fire did not consume the house, then the charge would not be made public, but if the fire burned rapidly and the blaze spread and was not put out before the dreamer awoke, then the charges would be made public.

We live everyday surrounded by mysteries and magick. Use the techniques described in this book to the benefit of not only yourself, but also to the benefit of those who live in this reality with you. For by helping others, you help yourself. We are all one in this mystical universe, and the wonders of our magickal world await us all.

You are indeed blessed.

DRAGONSTAR'S PERSONAL SERVICES AND PRODUCTS

Guaranteed to TAKE THE MYSTERY out of the MYSTICAL. . .

 #1 ☐ **DRAGONSTAR'S DESTINY READING AND SPELL KIT**

Have you ever dreamt of the day when your life would be straightened out and everything would return to "normal." In order for this to happen it is necessary to know what the cosmos holds in store for you. For while Dragonstar teaches that we are the master of our own destiny, sometimes it is necessary to have "expert" guidance and advice in order to walk the right path and to obtain your own "primary position" in the cosmos.

Along with a complete DESTINY READING which will assist in charting your path, Dragonstar will personally provide you with a "spell kit" for use in conjunction with your forecast and reading. It will be necessary for you to provide your birth information and two questions in your own handwriting which carries your vibrations with it.

Dragonstar's DESTINY READING is individual and personal and will provide you with key information to get you up and running in the New Millennium. Here is your chance to forge ahead at a time when great changes -- both personal and global -- are transpiring all around us. *$100*

DESTINY READING & SPELL KIT, ~~$75.00~~ (plus $4 shipping)

#2 ☐ **DRAGONSTAR'S LIFE STUDY COURSE**

NOW YOU CAN GRADUATE FROM THE MYSTIC LODGE OF DRAGONSTAR AND RECEIVE A DEGREE IN METAPHYSICS

The Mystic Lodge of Dragonstar is an ancient secret school with its lineage in Atlantis and Lemuria. Now the present day head of the lodge, Dragonstar, has been instructed to pass the teachings of the lodge on to a limited number of new students who wish to master the science of the occult. The teachings of the lodge will be passed down in the form of a monthly Study Course. Each month the enrolled student will receive a series of instructions and a questionnaire to be sent back to the lodge for grading. At the end of the 12 month Study Course all graduating students will receive a Degree as a Bishop in Metaphysics and a proclamation entitling them to instruct others in the way of the mystical.

The Dragonstar Life Study Course will include an in-depth study of:
● Reawakening your psychic abilities. ● Preparing for spiritual awakening. ● Becoming receptive to the Universe. ● The mystic power of words. ● The use of magick oils and incense. ● Developing hidden powers from within. ● Crystal power -- the energy of life. ● Candle magick - a personal guide. ● Learning to read the past, the present and future. ● Contacting the Ascended Masters for counseling and advice.

A limited number of students are now being accepted.
Enrollment cost $100 for the 12 month Life Study Course

FORTHCOMING BOOKS BY DRAGONSTAR*

* Please check where you bought this book for future release dates for these items,

■ CANDLE MAGICK: FROM CRYSTALS TO GEMSTONES

This absorbing title links the divine world of precious gemstones and crystals with the centuries old craft of candle burning magick. Most mystical gemstones and crystals were born of fire in antiquity. Learn how candle burning magick can resurrect this ancient energy in your stones to enhance their amazing abilities. This book is for those who are fascinated with the power and beauty contained in crystals & gems. ISBN: 1-892062-41-0

■ CANDLE BURNING MAGICK – ASTROLOGY & YOUR SUN SIGN

This book takes the reader on an amazing voyage of self-discovery as the true, but often suppressed, meaning of our birth dates are shown in connection with our true place in the universe. Also disclosed are methods of ancient candle burning magick and spell casting that employ the reader's personal sun sign and other astrological mysteries. Spells for love, money, protection and ways to personal happiness and success are discussed in a no-nonsense, easy-to-follow fashion that strip away deliberate deceit and obscurity. ISBN: 1892062-42-9

*OTHER ITEMS OF INTEREST

■ **INVISIBILITY AND LEVITATION: HOW TO KEYS TO PERSONAL PERFORMANCE** by Commander X Utilized by occultists, the military and martial artists. You can learn to perfect the ancient arts of levitation and invisibility that dates back to the time when the pyramids were constructed with a technology that we are only beginning to rediscover in the New Millennium. Here are practical experiments and NOT parlor tricks. $15.00

■ **TIME TRAVEL: A HOW-TO INSIDERS GUIDE** by Commander X with Tim Swartz Now it is possible to visit the past or the future with little know safe and proven methods!. Learn secrets utilized by the ancient scribes and mystics to benefit your own life.

■ **CANDLE BURNING WITH THE PSALMS** BY William Alexander Oribello

Did you known that each Psalm in the Holy Bible has a corresponding candle burning ritual that you can use for personal spiritual growth and everyday benefits of luck, love and money? Easy to read and USE! $12.00
Note: Books are available from your favorite book dealer or direct from the publisher: Inner Light Publications, Box 753, New Brunswick, NJ 08901 (732) 602-3407 -- our 24 hour automated credit card hot line.